Mel,
Hope you find this book of interest.
All the best for 2008.
Kind Regards
Maitland.

What More Philosophers Think

D1149385

Also available from Continuum:

What More **Philosophers Think**

Edited by Julian Baggini and Jeremy Stangroom

continuum

Continuum International Publishing Group
The Tower Building
11 York Road
London SE1 7NX
www.continuumbooks.com

80 Maiden Lane
Suite 704
New York
NY 10038

British Library Cataloguing-in-Publication Data
A catalogue record for this book is available from the British Library.

ISBN: HB: 0826492991
                9780826492999
          PB: 0826493009
                9780826493002

Library of Congress Cataloging-in-Publication Data
What More Philosophers Think/edited by Jeremy Stangroom and Julian Baggini. p. cm.

ISBN-13: 978-0-8264-9299-9
ISBN-10: 0-8264-9299-1
ISBN-13: 978-0-8264-9300-2
ISBN-10: 0-8264-9300-9
1. Philosphers – Interviews.   2. Philosophy, Modern.   I. Stangroom, Jeremy.   II. Baggini, Julian. III. Title.

B804.W43 2007
190.9'0511-dc22

2006034119

Typeset by BookEns Ltd, Royston, Herts.
Printed and bound in Great Britain by MPG Books Ltd, Bodmin, Cornwall

Contents

Acknowledgements

Many thanks to Sarah Douglas and her team at Continuum. To Ophelia Benson, Jonathan Derbyshire, and everybody else who has helped with *The Philosophers' Magazine* project. And, of course, to the philosophers who appear in this volume.

Preface

It is a common idea about philosophy that it is somehow divorced from the concerns of everyday life; that its protagonists are introverted characters much more at home perusing dusty volumes in great libraries than engaging with the realities of the world. The interviews in this volume show this idea up as the myth that it undoubtedly is. The subjects covered here include: terrorism, punishment, multiculturalism, party politics, cloning, medical consent and artificial intelligence.

This emphasis on social and political issues is in part a function of the history of these interviews. They were originally published in *The Philosophers' Magazine* between 2001 and 2005. Consequently, they took place in the context of the events of 11 September 2001, and the 'war on terror' which followed as a result. Thus, one finds the philosophers here wrestling with the question of philosophy's relevance in a world that is seemingly riven with strife. Although their conclusions are rarely bullish, the importance of philosophy as a way of engaging with the world is evident in their very act of considering its relevance.

For the most part this is a book of interviews. It is, however, worth saying something briefly about the exceptions. We have included two roundtable discussions. These both have a particular focus: the events of 11 September, and philosophy's response to the new security measures introduced in the UK as part of the 'war on terror'. We have also included something called 'The Soho Symposium'. Its subject is love, and its debt to Plato is entirely intentional.

The material in this book is arranged thematically. However, each chapter is self-contained, and can be read in isolation from the other chapters. The tone of the interviews is deliberately conversational in the sense that we have not sought to change the vocal register to ape an academic style. Obviously there has been some tidying up for reasons of grammar and syntax, but these remain interviews, and should be viewed as such.

Although a lot of the material here has been published before, this book is not simply a rehash. Many of the interviews have been extended with material that could not be included in the original versions due to restrictions of space. All of the material here has been polished up to make it suitable for the more permanent format of a book.

At the end of the introduction to *What Philosophers Think*, our first volume of Continuum interviews, we expressed the hope that the book would be of longer-lasting interest than most journal articles. We have exactly the same hope for this book.

Julian Baggini
Jeremy Stangroom
London, September 2006

1   Politics and Philosophy

Oliver Letwin

Imagine, if you will, President George W. Bush or Prime Minster Tony Blair giving a speech which contained a line like, 'The Kantian half of the truth about virtue and vice is that they are chosen; the Aristotelian half of the truth about virtue and vice is that they are learned.' It's not literally unimaginable – it's just that the chances of its actually happening are negligible.

Yet there is a senior British politician who uttered just those words in a political speech. He wasn't bluffing or taking the credit for the erudition of his speechwriter. The person who spoke these words knew what he was talking about, because he was a philosopher before he became a politician.

The Conservative Member of Parliament Oliver Letwin followed the old-fashioned route to high office: Eton, then Cambridge. His brief stint as an academic philosopher was as a fellow of Darwin College, Cambridge from 1981–1983. In 1987 he published a book of serious philosophy, *Ethics, Emotion and the Unity of Self*. But by the time it came out he had already left academe and was in the thick of politics.

Between 1983 and 1986 he was a member of Margaret Thatcher's policy unit. Then in 1987 he won the parliamentary seat of Dorset West, and in 2001 he rose to the front benches, having been appointed by Iain Duncan Smith to the post of

Shadow Home Secretary. In 2003, he climbed even further, as Michael Howard made him Shadow Chancellor of the Exchequer. His recent move to the lesser role of Shadow Secretary of State for Environment, Food and Rural Affairs seems not to be a demotion, but was at least in part down to a personal choice to concentrate more on his family. The more cynical suggest that he might be biding his time, aiming to challenge for the leadership of his party when it looks more likely to form a government.

With this intriguing and unusual biography, Letwin is uniquely placed to offer a view on the issue of social justice that is both philosophically informed and politically viable. Yet the mixing of his philosophical and political selves is far from straightforward, as we shall see.

When I spoke to Letwin at his office in Westminster's Portcullis House, I asked him what he thought the key issue of social justice was.

'I think the main question we need to be addressing is how we can have a society in which people grow up to be the kind of people that we would all like to be. That isn't the way it's often put, but it's my view of what it means to live in a socially just society. To my mind, something has gone very wrong – so we're doing a great social injustice – if there are people growing up to be the kind of people we wouldn't like to be: people who find themselves with chaotic lifestyles which they can't control and which drive them to despair and suicide; people who are oppressed by a lack of ability to control their world and deal with it; people who are deprived of a culturally rich existence: all these things seem to me profound social injustices.

'Some of them have to do with material prosperity, although that's never a guarantee of getting where I want people to be able to get to; nor is its absence a guarantee of not being able to get people where I want people to be able to get to. There are relationships, but it isn't the case that they should be conceived as a sort of mechanical operation for making sure that everybody has enough money, or for making sure that nobody is attacked by a burglar. It's something much deeper than either of those.'

Letwin agreed when I suggested that that sounded a lot like an Aristotelian conception of human flourishing. Yet, as he intimated, this is not what people usually think of when they hear the words 'social justice'. What tends to spring to mind are issues about distribution of wealth, and making sure it is fair. In contrast, when Letwin talks about social justice he is more concerned with what he called 'The Neighbourly Society', the title he gave to his collected speeches 2001–2003, covering the period he served as Shadow Home Secretary. This conception of justice has social order at its core. As he put it in one speech, 'the only just society is a crime-free society'. But does that mean redistribution of wealth does not come into his thinking at all? His answer might come as some surprise.

'I wrote a book called *The Purpose of Politics* in which I tried to work out what relation Rawlsian or other distributive conceptions of justice or policy had to prosperity, virtue, beauty and other desirable ends in politics. I came to believe that because politics should really be about trying to foster a civilized existence, each of these things is a value, and no one has supremacy – it isn't an either/or exercise. So I think that distributive justice of some form – and I'm actually quite attracted to Rawlsian views of what distributive justice amounts to – is one value, so is the value of prosperity, so is the value of beauty, so is the value of justice in a criminal sense. I don't see any one of these as supreme and I don't believe that there are permanent solutions to balancing these off. I see politics therefore as something that ought to be a process of continuous readjustment of the balance between a series of values, no one of which has primacy.'

This talk of different values, none of which is a master value, owes a great deal to the pluralism of Isaiah Berlin, which Letwin acknowledges. Does that then mean that Letwin, a senior Tory, can imagine a hypothetical situation in which the economic distribution in the country is much more uneven than it is now, in which he'd favour some sort of redistribution?

'Yes, yes, absolutely. Well I do favour continuous redistribution anyway. In fact every major political party in Britain at the moment does, and sponsors an enormous amount of it. But I could imagine circumstances in which increasing the level of redistribution became a primary goal. I can also imagine circumstances in which it was not at all the primary goal because a lot of that was going on, but something else was going very wrong. I don't see these things as permanent. I see them as constantly shifting.'

So the differences between the political parties is not so much that each holds different values, but rather has a lot to do with which one of those values they lay the greatest emphasis on.

'At any given moment,' he qualifies. 'Precisely the argument I make in that book is that it is not the case that Mr X wants something which is the exact opposite of what Mr Y wants. It is rather that Mr X and Mr Y will actually share in great part a series of values, but for one reason or another at a given moment one person is emphasizing one rather than the other. And the business of politics in a liberal democracy is the resolution of that particular issue.'

Right now, economic inequality is low on Letwin's list of priorities. At the top are those Aristotelian concerns about arranging society so as to enable people to become their best selves.

'I think there is at the moment a paradox that certain kinds of activity where it would be better if they were freer are more constrained; and other kinds of things where it would better if there were more social support or where social solidarity has been left to decline. For example, we live in a society where there is a huge aversion to risk. There is a colossal amount of regulation designed to minimize risk, I think to an extent which is impeding excellence, exuberance, cultural richness and so on. On the other side, people are growing up in circumstances where they are cruelly deprived of the emotional support that a human being needs in order to live the kind of life that many of us want to lead. This is a particularly intrusive state in some respects and a particularly thin society in other respects.'

Even though our conversation is philosophical, Letwin resists attempts to suggest that philosophy may actually have helped shape these views. He declines to name individual philosophers that he finds most attractive, saying, 'I don't think philosophers line up that way.' More seriously, perhaps, he refuses to entertain the notion that many of his political ideas rest on philosophical premises. For example, the autonomy of the self is clearly an important part of Letwin's social conservatism. And if he values the human capacity to choose freely, surely he must, as a philosopher, have some supporting views on the metaphysics of freedom? But, no, apparently.

'Issues of free will of the most profound, philosophical kind don't have much to do with addressing practical questions of our own lives or social organization.'

But, I insist, since he believes it is politically important that people should be treated as, and enabled to maximize themselves as, autonomous free agents, his position would only make sense under a certain understanding of human nature, and fundamentally the nature of the self.

'Yes, absolutely,' he says, before dodging the deeper philosophical disputes again. 'If I didn't believe that people are capable of making decisions and that it makes sense to hold people responsible for their decisions, then more or less everything else that I believe also wouldn't be believable. But I don't think anybody should delude themselves into imagining that they don't believe people make free decisions, or that they don't believe people should be held responsible for their decisions.'

I say I find it hard to believe that, given he was immersed in philosophy, his views on freedom had not in some way been shaped by philosophy.

'No-no-no-no-no, I resist that entirely,' he says, before I can finish the question. 'It is not the case that the reason why I think that we ought to do politics as if people were able to take decisions and be held responsible for them is because I have some philosophical preconception about how people are. On the contrary, this seems to me just blindingly obvious, and you don't need to be any kind of philosopher at all to recognize it. In fact people of all kinds recognize it every day of their lives all the time, and that's why they blame their children when they act wrongly and get cross with people who do things they don't think they should do.

'It is certainly the case that there are issues about how philosophically we deal with this brute fact alongside the brute fact that we are machines and that there are laws of physics. I accept that is a profound philosophical nexus of issues, but it's not a practical issue for moral life or political life.'

How separate then are Letwin's political and philosophical selves?

'I think that the only real connection between the two in my own case – and I may be deluding myself – is that habits of thought formed in the one inevitably get applied to the other. Whether it's beneficial for a politician to have a philosophical habit of thought, I don't know, but anyway I have one. The answer is that there ought to be people who do politics in that way and there ought to be people who do politics in quite other ways, and these people ought to be mixed, because, after all, politics is so death-defyingly difficult that people ought to come to it from very different perspectives.'

This echoes some comments he made back in 2003 at the British Academy, in a discussion co-organized with *The Philosophers' Magazine*. There, Letwin said that the benefit of philosophy is that it could raise the level of debate: 'As I see it, the biggest single problem of democracy in Britain today is the level of political discourse rather than the substance of the positions taken.'

'Yes, I do think that,' he confirms. 'I don't think this is unique to philosophy, but I think that any deep immersion in a serious academic discipline leads people to learn habits of thought that tend to raise levels of discourse. Philosophy is perhaps particularly well adapted to that because it is about thinking about matters of great complexity. That's a particularly good thing for talking about politics in a dispassionate, rational, careful fashion, which helps. It doesn't get the whole way to any answer, but it helps.'

It is interesting that Letwin is not better known as a philosopher. In countries like France, Spain or Germany it would be considered a great asset for a politician to be a philosopher. Does he think that in this country it's almost a disadvantage to confess a philosophical background?

'Massive,' he says, without hesitation. 'I do my best to conceal it.'

So why does it put people off?

'There's a good side and a bad side to that. The good side is that this country is a robustly commonsensical sort of place in which people distrust over-intellectualizing. After all, it's possible to intellectualize yourself into the gas chambers. The bad side to that is this is also a country in which there is a sort of excessive distaste for intellectuals, and there's something good about a country like France where people came out in the streets when Sartre died, which certainly wouldn't happen in England.'

For now, Letwin's thoughtful approach to politics has retreated from the front line. One can't help wondering, however, what would happen if Letwin did return to try to lead his party. What would Britain make of a philosopher-ruler in waiting?

Suggested Reading

The Neighbourly Society (Centre for Policy Studies)
The Purpose of Politics (The Social Market Foundation)

In the autumn of 2001, at the invitation of *The Philosophers'*
Magazine, the philosophers Jonathan Rée, Anthony O'Hear,
Jennifer Hornsby and David Conway participated in a roundtable
discussion on the appropriate philosophical response to the
events of 11 September 2001.

In what way, if any, do the events of 11 September and their
aftermath demand or invite a distinctly philosophical response?
Rée: I think there is a pretty sharp distinction between those
who have simply used 11 September as an occasion to explain
how right they've always been in their analysis of everything; and
those – a fairly large number, I suspect – who have really taken
it seriously as an event which opens out a new space of political
and philosophical possibilities, scope both for new hope and for
new fears. I think it may prove to be an event of the same order
as 14 July 1789 – that people may still be wondering whether
the event and its consequences were on the whole progressive
or on the whole disastrous two hundred years later, just as they
are with the storming of the Bastille.

The reasons why it might seem to be an event which thoroughly
upsets people's political concepts is nothing to do with the scale of
it. As many people have pointed out, the death of a few thousand

people in New York does not count for much statistically, compared with the 20 million innocent civilians who have been killed in wars in the past ten years. I think you can get an idea of what's novel about it by trying to imagine the state of mind of the people who flew the planes, particularly into the World Trade Center. Picture them waiting in the departure lounge, with the people they were about to kill milling around them. Picture the little kids wandering around, coming up to them and trying to engage them in conversation, as kids do. Obviously there have been bombers who have killed more people, at Hiroshima, for example. But somehow or other, perhaps through self-delusion, they didn't have to be in a state of vindictive personal hatred when they did it; indeed they probably thought they were doing it out of love of humanity and peace. It seems to me this does make a big difference.

Conway: I don't know if philosophers have any particular insight into it, but I've been very interested in trying to work out, or to see if anyone is capable of working out, the nature of the states of mind of the people who perpetrate such acts, both at the times they commit them and also in the lead up to their doing so. I gather that they're not all as they were originally characterized – uneducated lads who had been brainwashed – but they were quite educated, often highly educated.

Hornsby: I agree broadly speaking with what's been said, but I'm actually doubtful whether philosophers have any particular expertise in understanding their states of mind. I'm also doubtful that one should spend a lot of time trying to think about their states of mind and understanding them better. Maybe it's enough to say that they were fanatics who loved what strikes most of us as evil. I don't think philosophers can get much beyond that. It's not so much their individual states of mind but the background to them – the states of mind of millions of people in the world – that's a far more interesting question.

I think events have created a moment to think, and since philosophers are thinkers they should be thinking. But I actually suspect that it's a relatively small area in which we have any special expertise.

Conway: Like some people here I'm uncertain as to what distinctive contribution professional Anglo-American philosophers can make. This is not what we've spent our lives thinking about. Perhaps now we're going to be forced to address issues to do with how the globe is to be cohabited, if it is to be cohabited, by sets of people with such seemingly mutually irreconcilable worldviews.

O'Hear: I was struck by the reference to the French Revolution because I think this is or will be a turning point in people's mentality in a number of respects. Burke wrote that on the tomb of the murdered monarchy of France had arisen a terrible phantom, unappalled by peril, unchecked by remorse, and despising all common maxims and all common means. That, I think, is a good definition of terror, and after all terror was first implemented as a policy in the French Revolution. It seems to me that we in the west have been far too tolerant of terrorism for the last 50 or so years. I find it shameful the way we continually give way to IRA terrorism. I don't doubt for one minute that bin Laden and people like that are aware that terrorists tend to win. It seems to me that people who adopt terror as their means are beyond reasonable discussion and therefore the only way to deal with them is to engage them in some kind of war, if you can find them, of course.

There is a philosophical point here which is the just war doctrine, which is probably more honoured in the breach than the observance. It not only insists that the cause is just – *jus ad bellum* – but that it is fought justly – *jus in bello*. Because terrorists have no regard for *jus in bello* – they actually want to use the demoralization and destruction of non-combatants and innocents – therefore the just war doctrine bears directly against terrorism. That means that in defending oneself against terrorism one has to be more scrupulously careful than one sometimes is about *jus in bello*.

It's interesting that there has been some agreement here that there's not much professional philosophers specifically can say about 11 September and its aftermath. What does that say about philosophy as it is practised in the Anglophone world?

Rée: I think it may lead to progress. Quite a lot of people have been asking, 'Where are the public intellectuals?' and in particular 'Where is the Bertrand Russell of the year 2001?' Now I think – and speak as a leftist, and a pretty extreme one in present company – that Bertrand Russell was a disaster politically and philosophically when he set himself up as a political expert. It was fatuous of him to fire off telegrams to all these politicians – people like Kennedy, Mao, Castro, De Gaulle – and to expect people to pay attention to him because he was a man of reason and he spoke on behalf of the survival of humanity, whereas they were merely politicians concerned with worldly power. I think he made a self-righteous idiot of himself and I suspect he did more harm than good.

I've been reading some of Leibniz's correspondence recently, and he was keenly aware, unlike Russell, of the fact that politics calls for delicate balancing acts: there's not much point in preaching principles, you have to make alliances. But look at what Russell says about Leibniz in *The History of Western Philosophy*: that Leibniz is the kind of person one would choose as a servant because he's loyal and flexible and has no real ideas of his own. Leibniz, we are to understand, was not a genuine philosophical freethinker like Russell. It seems to me that Leibniz provides a much better model for a philosopher intervening in politics than Russell ever could.

Hornsby: I think the point is that philosophy is not the same as military studies, Middle East studies, US studies, political theory, international law and so on. There are all sorts of fields where experts might know stuff which is relevant, and of course one hopes that any decisions that will be made will be wise, and one hopes that philosophers are wise. But it's not only philosophers who aspire to be wise. So I can feel quite comfortable with the idea that philosophers don't have anything distinctive to say: it seems to me that all the facts that need to be got in aren't things that we're especially well-placed to know.

O'Hear: I think that it was not only Russell that made a fool of himself when he brought philosophy into politics. Almost every philosopher who's spoken on political matters in the past half-century that I can remember, such as Sartre, they've all been catastrophically wrong. The more certain they've been the more wrong they've been. I think that the wisdom that philosophy should articulate is a wisdom which is available to everybody. It's not that philosophers have a particular entrée to do it, it's just that we do it more systematically or reflectively. So you wouldn't expect philosophers to say things different from other people. This is an Aristotelian point, that the philosopher's practical wisdom is the recapitulation of the experience of the many and the wise.

Conway: I think there has been a useful philosophical lesson which is capable of being drawn from the appalling tragedy of 11 September, and I think it is a belated appreciation among many Anglo-American philosophers of just how wonderful the open, free democratic societies of America and Britain have been and are which they have ritually castigated for the past 30 years. They might have belatedly woken up to the vulnerability in which they've been placed, not least in part by the rhetoric which has spewed forth since 1968.

Rée: I don't think David need worry: philosophy as a whole has been solidly and securely right-wing and considerably libertarian in the last 30 years. I don't think that leftist anti-Americanism has been exactly the majority view.

Hornsby: My sense is that the American public and to some extent the British public has come to appreciate the kind of ignorance they have had about the world. They've been happy to go along with, and not even to know much about, the kind of isolationism which has come to characterise the US. There's now a kind of wake-up call. So far from feeling how very privileged they've been, they may be thinking how very unfortunate it is that these questions haven't been addressed.

Do you think 11 September has had any impact on the intellectual life of philosophers?

Rée: The other day I was talking to the distinguished political philosopher Catherine Audard, who has devoted vast energies to introducing American liberalism to Continental Europe in recent years. If I understood her rightly, she was saying that 11 September was one of the worst intellectual shocks she had ever suffered. She had been working to expand the space in which liberal rationality could be operative in political decision-making and she was now beginning to fear she had been living in cloud-cuckoo land, because that space has proved to be so fragile.

O'Hear: It is true, rather, that *civilization* is fragile and the norms and institutions needed to sustain it can easily be subverted and the more liberal they are, the easier it is to subvert them. You could call this a philosophical lesson.

Hornsby: I don't know if others saw something which was put out by a US academic trade union saying that the events were tragic and deplorable. Then there was a statement about how they set great store by free speech and the democratic principles by which they lived, and how these flourished in the university environment. The message was that we academics must do what we can to ensure this free atmosphere prevails. I confess that when I saw this, it seemed to me ironic that they could be celebrating their love of free speech and democracy, when you might think what they need to do is reflect on how little they actually knew about the background to this event, and that in a genuinely open society, they presumably would have known better about what their government was doing in their name.

Have any of our most fundamental notions about philosophy been undermined by these events, such as the power of rational reflection to change people's ideas? Is this a fundamental strike at the philosophical project because we can't see how this act can be motivated by someone committed to the role of rationality in our lives?

Hornsby: I would say that there is a lesson about the limits of reason. I take it we're all liberals around this table, some more libertarian than others, and we have been taught to value truth and reason and the accessibility of truth and reason to people at large. But I think what we've seen is that this has its limitations.

O'Hear: It certainly has its limitations with people who are not prepared to engage in rational discussions, but this is something which has been pointed out, not least by philosophers, that the open society is vulnerable to force. My reaction to that is that we have to be not only more vigilant, but more prepared to stand up, if necessary, in a military way. That of course would be the triumph of the terrorist, since one thing the terrorists want is for the liberal society to be repressive. They want to force that.

Conway: I think it would be naïve and simplistic to think that Muslim fundamentalism exhibits defects of rational capacity greater than that which is exhibited by anyone who subscribes to any form of revealed religion. As far as Muslims are concerned, Mohammed was privy to a revelation which was authenticated by miracles that were no less confirming of it than Christians believe *a propos* of Jesus and Jews do of Moses. Unless you're going to say of anyone who subscribes to any form of revealed religion that they're beyond the pale rationally speaking, then one has then to consider whether or not it is possible with respect to a Muslim to demonstrate to them beyond reasonable doubt why what they purport to be a revelation is inferior. No doubt westerners think they can do this, but I'll give credit to Rawls for supposing that there are limits to that agenda, of one comprehensive doctrine being shown to be rationally superior to any other.

Hornsby: When I said that reason has its limits, my thought was that if you want to regulate the lives of people who share the planet, you cannot appeal to principles of reason alone as interpreted by western liberal democracies.

Rée: I think we may be facing a deeper philosophico-political transformation; not about whether rationality can prevail over irrationality, but about historicity and historicism. I think most kinds of progressive and optimistic political thought in the twentieth century were buoyed up by an assumption that deep historical events must have deep historical roots; and that in the long run most people will reach a reasonable appreciation of the true principles of human society so that history will ensure that in the end good will prevail and all manner of things will be well. But it's quite possible that the perpetrators of the events of 11 September represented only a tiny fraction of world opinion and sentiment, and that they would have remained obscure and ineffectual if only some individual in the CIA had been a bit cleverer and foiled the attack. Maybe one great philosophical benefit of 11 September will be a renewed sense of the sheer contingency of history.

Hornsby: I agree that it is utterly contingent that there was that event on 11 September, but what it drew our attention to was a great evil in the world. There's a sense of injustice from which millions and millions of people, most of them Muslims, suffer, and which most people in the west had very little awareness of. Some of this sense of injustice is internal to the regimes, some is directed specifically at the west. This wasn't widely known and this is now widely known. So it seems to me that there is a great historical significance to the events of 11 September.

Are there any other questions which philosophers should be thinking about in the aftermath of 11 September?

Rée: There has been a certain kind of philosophical formalism about discussion of politics, and especially international relations, in recent years – especially since the end of the cold war. The main criteria of just action have been sought in issues of legality or international right. The justification for bombing Iraq, for example, was supposed to be the violation of the national sovereignty of Kuwait; but 50 years earlier, perhaps even ten years earlier, the question would have been one of evaluating the forces at play and you find the ones that are going to produce the kind of future that you want. And I suspect that the contrast between a past-oriented and a future-oriented approach to political justification has been sharpened by the events of 11 September. If there is going to be a conceptual reconstruction then perhaps it will involve resuscitating the question of what kind of future we want to create, and spending less time making heavy weather of the past.

Conway: I think if this event does anything for professional philosophers, it should give them occasion to consider undertaking a radical revision of what passes for the philosophy curriculum. I think we're way too insular, I think we're way too parochial and we have abandoned any serious attempt in the last century to grapple with these sorts of cultural issues.

Hornsby: There is a question about British universities in general and the nature of the education students get, which is whether there shouldn't be more opportunity one way or another for them to learn to be informed citizens, so that they can show wisdom when it comes to international events of this sort. It's not utterly clear to me that it's specifically for philosophers to make the opportunities. Perhaps we need something more resembling a liberal education.

3   Security and the 'War on Terror'

Philosophers Tony McWalter, Catherine Audard, Saladin Meckled-García, Alex Voorhoeve and Jonathan Rée discuss philosophy's response to the new security measures introduced in the UK as part of the 'war on terror'.

What has been your general impression of the measures introduced in the UK as part of the 'war on terror', such as detention without trial and control orders?

McWalter: The incredible rush to legislate on such matters in a matter of days in the UK is completely anti-philosophical. One of the things you expect a philosopher to do is to see not only the consequences of a proposal, but the consequences of the consequences; and even the consequences of the consequences of the consequences. That's why we do philosophy, because policy has unobvious repercussions. Given that policy on terrorism is such a difficult area, to take executive decisions about what the legal framework is going to be within a very short time is itself deeply invidious to the welfare of society and the liberty of its subjects.

Isn't it a little precious of philosophers to say 'We need to take our time and think things through'? Isn't it a political necessity that sometimes things do have to be dealt with quickly?

Audard: The rush itself is not a drawback. What is important is the inclusion of a sunset clause, so that any legislation on those matters has to stop at one stage and be re-enacted and reconsidered again. That's crucial.

Meckled-García: It's quite right that under certain circumstances governments, executives and legislatures have to take measures which are emergency sensitive. But that has to be balanced against two other factors. One is the scale of the threat: how large is the imminent danger? And also there has to be a level of proportionality. I think the more draconian the measures, the more you have to think about how hasty the legislation is. In this case I think the measures that were proposed were so out of proportion – especially as they contravened the Convention of Human Rights and other civil liberties standards – that the haste was indecent.

Voorhoeve: I wonder if the problem is not the government's haste, but instead the belief that the government will not, on balance, lose votes in the next election by appearing to be tough on terror. The government will therefore intentionally push the boundaries and take controversial measures. But we should be reluctant to limit rights that have withstood the test of time, that have proven to be good solutions to perennial social problems. Limiting the right of *habeas corpus* and allowing secret evidence, as is happening in the case of control orders, for example, shows a lack of respect for tested ways of ensuring that detention is justified.

None of this so far suggests that any of the measures themselves are actually wrong, or that there are any principled objections to them, only that they've been brought in too hastily.

McWalter: The issue is not the measures, it's the evidence-base on which those individuals are selected to be the objects of those measures. We all know, particularly in the age of George Bush, how lamentable governments can be, and how wrong their systems can be. Post the Iraq war we all know how rotten the briefings which are meant to give them the information on which they take these decisions can be.

Voorhoeve: The principle is this: we should be very careful about effectively giving officials power to punish people without proper checks. We don't have to believe in ill intent or recklessness on the part of government in order to consider this an important principle. It's just that mistakes are very often made, as intelligence on Iraq and other cases show.

Audard: I think we need to remember the notion of civil liberties where security is a basic right. If people could understand national interest or national security in more convincing ways, then the threat of terrorism would make more sense. Instead in Britain we see it as a conflict between *raison d'état* – of the state and the executive – and civil liberties. Things are not like that. Liberty without security is meaningless. Beyond the conflict, the aim should be about including reasonable access to security within our framework of civil liberties and reaching a balance instead of rushing into conflicts of principles. A measure of pragmatism is important. Do the preventive measures have reasonable chances of success? Probably not. This should be explained too: what minimal level of security can democracies provide their citizens? How much extra or non-derogatory power does the state need to meet these new risks? Information and public debate about calculated risks should have happened prior to the legislation to avoid hysteria. But this would be too philosophical.

McWalter: I think it is wrong for the government to take non-derogatory powers. A power is derogatory if it is subject to independent assessment, which may conclude that a minister took a decision against an individual which he or she should not have done. A non-derogatory power says 'I'm going to make this decision as Home Secretary and I am not responsible to anybody and nobody is going to oversee this.' That is in my view the weakness of the 2005 legislation. The overall consequence is that we have a power which has never been implemented, but it shows the tip of an iceberg – that there is constant move towards a non-derogatory system rather than a derogatory one.

Audard: But the difficulty is that we are trying to prevent terrorism, not simply to clean up afterwards, and that is a difficult grey area. We are giving non-derogatory powers to prevent terrorism, and that's really tricky.

McWalter: We have a strong system built up over generations, which has immense wisdom about how we try to reconcile these different aims; if you're faced with a new threat you seek a new statement of what you do to continue that tradition but to apply it in new ways. Non-derogatory powers went well beyond that and you wouldn't have arrived at the same legislation if someone had been given a proper chance to say, 'Hang on a minute, this is going to affect innocent people in ways which are far too detrimental not just to their interests but the interests of the wider society.'

Rée: This is beginning to look like old Labour meets Burke. Tony is speaking like a traditionalist getting high on the aroma of old British ways. But they have been abridged often enough, for example, during the Second World War, much more severely than now, with the compulsory internment of enemy aliens. I'm afraid that if this is the kind of thing that philosophy wants to contribute to political discussion then it is not going to get very far: politicians would respond, 'That's all very well, but politics is about emergencies in which you have to balance one thing with another'. Talking about consequences of consequences of consequences is something that may make you feel very pleased with yourself, but remember that philosophers talked about consequences of consequences of consequences and found themselves solidly backing the Soviet Union, China and Nazi Germany.'

Meckled-García: I thought the consequences of consequences point was that the government continuously declares itself to be in favour of what it calls 'evidence-based policy-making', the idea that you really need to know what the policy does in terms of evidence, that you can show it works; yet in instances like this it comes out guns blazing. That was the point, rather than that philosophers should sit around thinking about consequences until the cows come home.

One thing that the government seems to be very good at doing is blurring traditional boundaries within the legal system, in particular the boundary between a suspect and somebody who's come through the courts and who has had their innocence tested. When you allow the status of 'suspect' to have such drastic penal consequences for the individual, you are blurring the boundaries between that concept and the concept of convicted criminal. I think there is a principled question there.

You say that people have blurred the boundaries between things like suspect and criminal. Maybe the reason they do that is that conceptual distinctions are never as neat in the real world as they are in theory. As soon as you enter the world of practice, you have to blur distinctions. You refuse to do so at your own peril.

Rée: Surely the problem is that until you've committed your terrorist act, like 9/11, you haven't actually committed a crime, and so you can't be treated in the same way as someone suspected of fraud or drug dealing. A drug dealer is committing a crime now. Someone planning a terrorist attack in a year's time isn't …

Voorhoeve: Yes they are – committing acts preparatory to terrorism and conspiracy to commit an act of terror are crimes.

McWalter: The point about needing 90 days to gather evidence is because there isn't any direct evidence in terms of, say, explosives, because the conspirators don't need such materials until the day before their planned action.

There is a topical example, actually. Recently Abu Hamza, the 'radical Muslim cleric', as he is usually described, was sentenced to seven years. It is so obvious now that the number of people who were involved in very actual and often horrific crimes who can be traced back to him is very large. Surely people who are going to defend what are called 'draconian measures' are going to say this is exactly an example of what happens if you are too afraid to take pre-emptive measures before the event. By the time you step in, by the time there's even a plot, it's too late.

McWalter: This is not relevant at all because Abu Hamza was committing acts which were illegal even under the 1861 act, and therefore you don't need new laws and statutes to cope with them. The fact that our security people were pussy-footing around is neither here nor there. You didn't need a new statute to deal with him, whereas in these other cases, as Jonathan has correctly said, you clearly do, because those who recruit suicide bombers actually get people who are completely clean in terms of their records. If you shoplifted as a fourteen-year-old you're not going to be a suicide bomber because you have a record somewhere in the system and they will pick you up. So potential recruits have to be completely clean and those who recruit know that they have enough people who are completely clean to carry out these acts.

Meckled-García: What's fascinating is that 'completely clean' reminds me of Meno's paradox, which is: how do you know what you're looking to find out unless you already know what it is; until you know the shape of the thing you are trying to investigate, how will you know you've found it? Crazily, being 'completely clean' can make you a suspect because no one knows which completely clean individual is a threat until they have committed a crime. Arrests, then, become random. You end up in the situation as in cases in the States where you had all these incarcerations, and only five people were eventually charged, and even the things they were prosecuted for were just passport inconsistencies and things like that.

Voorhoeve: I accept the need to stop people before they've committed an atrocity. That is probably what the terrorism bill has done well – to bring in a lot of new crimes which relate to planning and supporting terrorism. But once you have that, it's not clear to me that you also need a very long period of detention without charge on the basis that they haven't committed a terrorist act yet, since they may have committed one of these other offences.

So the dominant view seems to be that if you legislate against the right kinds of crime and the powers are derogatory, then you don't need the more draconian measures like detention without trial for extended periods.

Rée: It strikes me that one advantage of creating a non-derogatory power – if I've understood what it means – is that it then clearly belongs to an accountable minister. And it's actually quite a good idea that it should be someone who is nameable and responsible. It wouldn't be much better if it were done by an anonymous panel of experts.

Meckled-García: The point with non-derogatory powers is that they're just decisions which ministers make, and they can be made *in camera*, they can be completely secretive.

Voorhoeve: Reasons for government decisions should generally be made publicly accessible in terms which every reasonable citizen could understand and accept.

This is all checks and balances stuff. So imagine all the checks and balances are in place, with the proper things legislated against. Could we imagine a justifiable, well-drafted bill for 90-days' detention without trial, with derogatory powers?

Meckled-García: But if the right things are made illegal, if something warranted your being detained for 90 days, it would be recognized as a criminal offence.

Voorhoeve: None of us are saying, 'Under no circumstances could 90 days' detention be justified.' It's just that given the great importance of not giving government powers to punish people without putting the punishment through a court, the case has not been made.

Audard: I was wondering whether Britain would be better off with a written constitution, because the balance of power and the checks and balances would really be working. If we have the law lords saying, 'no way, that's impossible', there would nothing for us to protest against.

What about the laws concerning glorification, justification, promotion and fermenting of terrorism?

Audard: Advocacy of revolutionary and subversive doctrines is part of free speech and is allowed. But would glorification of terror fit into that category? That's not glorification of a doctrine, it's a glorification of means that leads to criminal activities, to inflicting death sentences on innocents, etc. Are these discourses completely disconnected from criminal acts? Are discourses in the void or should not the speaker or the author be held to account?

Meckled-García: I don't have a problem with fermenting, but normally a liberal principle of free speech is one that regards expressions of free speech to be available and permissible so long as those expressions don't themselves lead to a particular kind of consequence. So you don't judge an expression of free speech in terms of its content, you judge it in terms of its consequences.

This isn't just hypothetical. What would the law make of Ted Honderich's book After the Terror?

Meckled-García: That's a good example. Honderich continues to entertain the idea that some forms of what he identifies as terrorism – and incidentally it's a different definition – are in some instances justified. The Palestinians, in his words, are morally entitled to their terrorism. Now if the government or the appropriate body were to identify that as a statement which fits in with its definition, he would be a criminal. I think it would be quite likely that there would be individuals calling for the Crown Prosecution Service to prosecute him, because he is justifying certain forms of terrorist acts. I think that would be a mistake. If it can be shown that you're directing terror, that's an entirely different ball game, because you're talking about very specific consequences.

McWalter: I think your argument is in part to do with a perception in the wider society that philosophy is impotent, and hence it can be tolerated. Not all would agree. I think that it's very interesting that the Catholic church, when they ran the Index, the books they put on the top were philosophy books. Kant's *Critique of Pure Reason* was on the proscribed list until the list was itself abolished in 1967. The reality is that, if people think that if a case is really well argued – and I agree with Jonathan that philosophers don't have a monopoly on that – and if the view becomes absorbed into society, not always with people even explicitly reading the book, some people may say that's far more dangerous than some nutcase raving on the lawn outside Finsbury Park Mosque. Philosophers often are tolerated by society because we are seen as impotent; but following the conviction of Irving in Austria, where it is clear that the assumption that history is sociologically impotent has been rejected, there is a distinct possibility that the tabloid press in the UK can put a philosopher in the spotlight today, and the freedom of philosophers can be curtailed tomorrow. That is why Catherine was right to say we need a written constitution, for we should see such freedoms as defining our society.

That does seem to question the attempted distinction between incitement and justification. What you seem to be saying is that a justification for terrorism could do more to actually bring about terrorism than a random person standing on the street saying 'bomb the bastards'. The question is: can a sincerely argued justification for terrorism be seen as incitement and something which the law could justifiably punish? Imagine a law which criminalizes incitement but not justification specifically: could a justification be taken as incitement if it could be shown that that justification had consequences?

Audard: The reaction of some Muslims has been to say that of course many of those who are called terrorists in the west are in reality freedom fighters such as we have had in the past too in Europe or in the ex-colonies and so we should understand their glorification of terror as legitimate. That's a very strong form of justification, but it is unacceptable because the aim of terror is the prevention of any democratic form of conflict resolution.

Meckled-García: It's not about consequences or no

consequences. Any piece of writing can have consequences and they're often unpredictable. You can see why incitement has immediate and obvious consequences, it's telling people directly to do something. Giving a view that there are theoretical justifications why terrorism is sometimes justifiable – I'd like to see that, just like the current tracts that argue torture is justifiable, because you want to be able to engage the arguments and you want the public debate to continue on that basis. Now that might have consequences down the line.

Are there any other aspects of the legislative response to the terror threat that interest you?

Audard: My worry about all this concerns the perception of terror and what it means in a free society, compared to the kind of terror people experienced during the war. We mentioned terrible injustices, the internment of aliens in Britain, etc. I have a feeling that after 9/11 and 7/7, things have gone out of control, and that they should be brought into perspective with what Britain has been through with the Irish question. Historical awareness and public debates are important to help to assess the situation. My question is: are these new crimes? Are we really so vulnerable that we need entirely new measures? We are not sure enough of our principles – that Tony earlier labelled as strong and wise. The bases of democratic life are not really clear enough in this country, or in the liberal west in general.

Voorhoeve: Catherine talked about the continuities with the threat of the IRA and so on, but the current threat seems different. I don't think that the IRA had the intention of killing as many people as possible in Britain. It wanted attention for its cause, it wanted to push public opinion in a certain direction, but I cannot imagine that it was its intention to kill, if possible, 100,000 people in Britain.

Rée: I'm not convinced that there's that much of an overreaction to terrorism, though I'd agree that terrorism is too vague a word. Surely the basic question is whether or not the society we live in is under threat from Islamo-fascism. If it isn't then we need not get worried; but if it is then we need to think again.

I am worried by something that keeps coming up in our discussion: a general suspicion of the motives of politicians. I'm afraid that people like us are vacating the proper sphere of politics in the name of a kind of purism.

One thing we keep coming back to is that maybe this legislation isn't really necessary because there are already statutes which cover these offences. But the state is not like an academic committee devising a set of exam regulations. Legislation is a political act as well as a legal act and there can be reasons why it is proper for a state to introduce legislation that from a theoretical point of view may not be absolutely necessary. Legislation that repeats existing legislation can energise discussion.

And I would like to make a more general point about what's changed over the last twenty years: the rise of what I would call moralistic masochism: which is to say people scanning the political horizon in the hope of finding things which make them feel deeply depressed. We embrace bad news as a confirmation of our own moral discrimination. There's a wonderful remark that Kierkegaard makes about people producing political opinions not in order to contribute to discussion about what society should be like but to contribute to the image of their own moral praiseworthiness. It's happened among people who like to think of themselves as progressive in the west and it's the exact mirror image of certain kinds of fascistic movements particularly within the Islamic world, where radicalism thrives on bad news. If the protesting Islamists thought that the diffusion of those offensive cartoons was damaging what they hold dear they wouldn't have gone about their protests the way they have.

That's what I mean by moral masochism, and I call it moral because it seems to me to be turning every issue into one about individual righteousness rather than one about the collective interests of society. An elementary fact that philosophers should be deeply aware of is that political imperatives and moral imperatives often conflict, that moral imperatives often conflict with each other and that political imperatives sometimes have to be allowed to trump moral imperatives, quite apart from negotiating between them. And I'm afraid that the whole way we're approaching these discussions, and tearing out our hair about infringements of civil liberties, is part of a process in which the political field is being evacuated, political arguments are being removed from the political sphere and replaced with moralistic soap-boxing.

Meckled-García: I haven't seen any political theorist write any work in which they identify this autonomous area of the political which is somehow devoid or distinct from principles.

Rée: But moral principles are not the only kind of principles …

Meckled-García: If you mean practical principles of action, then I think that all practical principles of action, if they are going to motivate the organization of our social life, then have to at some point engage with morality and social principle. And if you want to say they are specific things called political principles then I think they're just a subset of moral principles.

Rée: Hannah Arendt has a neat way of distinguishing the political and the moral: the moral is about what kind of person you'd like to be and the political is about what kind of society we'd like to see.

Audard: The distinction does not make sense because as a person I have strong views about the kind of society I want to live in and the kind of good social life represents. Living in a democracy and not under state terror – or religious terrorism – means that my view of the good can translate into the political.

I'm sure we could go on much further, but we've run out of time, so we need to end it there.

4   Terrorism and Punishment

Ted Honderich

It is easy to think that there is no difficult issue about the justification of punishment. It seems just obvious, for example, that in the face of the horrors of 9/11 or the murders of two young schoolgirls at Soham, it is right that society should punish their perpetrators. However, when one begins to examine the details of the justifications of punishment more closely things rapidly become quite tricky. Consider, for example, the idea that people are responsible for their crimes. Supposing it turns out that a suicide bomber has been schooled from early childhood to believe that by blowing herself up in a busy market in Tel Aviv she is honouring God. Is she then blameworthy for her actions? Could she have known that what she was doing was wrong (if indeed it was wrong)? What if she had never been exposed to ideas that might have suggested that killing innocent bystanders is not acceptable? Does this make a difference?

These kinds of questions, and many others like them, make the topic of the justification of punishment one of enduring interest. Ted Honderich has examined the issues surrounding this topic for a new edition of his admirable forensic book *Punishment: The Supposed Justifications Revisited*. His central argument is that the standard justifications of punishment offered by philosophers are flawed in various ways. What, I ask him, are his objections to the retributive and utilitarian justifications of punishment?

'With respect to retributive justifications of punishment the question boils down to what sense you can give to this utterance: punishment is right because it is deserved,' he tells me. 'It seems to me that in the history of retribution theory no satisfactory meaning has ever been given to it. This might be thought to be a brave claim, but I'm inclined to think that it is true. The most obvious failings are those which equate "because it is deserved" with "because it is right", thereby introducing an absurd circularity. Of course, the circularity is sometimes concealed; that is, some account of retribution is given which is complicated and possibly elusive, but in the end you find that what it boils down to is precisely this circularity. For example, jurisprudents are inclined to say that punishment is right because it is linked to a worked-out system of penalties and offences. But at some point along the way they have to face up to the fact that their worked-out system of penalties and offences might not justify punishment at all, as was the case in Nazi Germany, for example. This possibility means that they will often speak of a "system of justice", which in effect is to say a justified system of penalties and offences, so the thing becomes circular.

'Alternative attempts to give sense to this argument of desert fail for other reasons. In the end, I find myself saying that there must be some sense in the retribution tradition – a large tradition of feeling, talk and action could not be entirely without sense – and this sense is that retribution gives satisfaction to people's grievance desires, their desire for the distress of offenders. This gives an exact sense to the notion of equivalence: it's just enough distress to satisfy desires and not too much. It also gives a general reason for punishment. The satisfaction of any desire is *a* reason, which, needless to say, may be overwhelmed by reasons against, which is indeed the case with retribution theory.

'As far as utilitarian theory is concerned,' Honderich continues, 'the central objection is almost an ancient one. If you follow the policy of maximizing satisfaction, going for the greatest total of satisfaction, with no question raised at all about its distribution, it is perfectly clear that there may be circumstances in which you produce the greatest satisfaction by unfair or vicious means. For example, it might be that it is the society with a few slaves which produces the greatest total of happiness. With respect to punishment, it just is the case that if you seek the end of the greatest reduction in offences, on occasion you might have to victimize somebody to do it. That's a longstanding objection to utilitarianism.'

It isn't clear why utilitarians can't simply bite a bullet here. In some circumstances, we think it is right to cause the innocent to suffer in the service of the greater good. Quarantine is perhaps the best example. Consider, for example, that during the great plague of 1665, whole villages would on occasion quarantine themselves, knowing perfectly well that the healthy as well as the sick would die as a result. So why not simply accept that sometimes it might be justified to punish an innocent person in the name of the greater good? Or to give a more specific and controversial example, why not simply bite the bullet that it might be right to torture an innocent person to death, if by doing so you prevent a nuclear holocaust?

'That's a perfectly reasonable rejoinder,' Honderich replies. 'Indeed, it is the case that we already victimize a lot. For example, we victimize people in the law: when we put people in jail for a certain class of offences, those where there is neither intent, nor negligence – strict liability cases – this is precisely an instance of victimizing people, and we think that it is worth it.

'So the objection to utilitarianism has to be sharpened up somewhat. You have to be clear that what is unacceptable is that utilitarianism can be made to justify torturing somebody to death on the grounds that what is gained from it is a greater total of satisfaction than the pain caused to the person being tortured, but where the distribution of satisfaction is such that the gain to any particular individual is trivial, such as the gain of having an extra cup of coffee, or something like that. Surely in that circumstance, torturing somebody to death is a monstrous act.'

Honderich's view is that whilst retribution theories of punishment are weak, they must have some content of argument in them. This argument, as we have seen, is that punishment satisfies grievance desires, and may do exactly that, no more and no less. One can see clear expression of this idea in the responses of victims and the families of victims to the perpetrators of the crimes that have affected them. Thus, for example, the aunt of murder victim Billie-Jo Jenkins is on record recently as saying 'We want justice for her, revenge is sweet.' However, it seems possible that the criticisms that are levelled against utilitarianism might also be levelled against the idea that punishment is justified by the satisfaction of grievances. Could we not satisfy grievances by victimizing?

'Yes,' agrees Honderich, 'it is true that the retribution theory on my construction is open to the kind of criticism that you're talking about here. You could indeed satisfy grievances by victimizing. This stuff about victimization, and utilitarianism justifying it, can sound a little bit unreal. But I'm not sure how unreal it is. We've got people in Belmarsh prison right now who haven't been convicted of anything, and it is very unclear what is to be gained by having them there.'

These kinds of thoughts dovetail with some of the issues that come up when one thinks about security and terrorism. If you're a utilitarian can you not simply say that increased security might well lead to innocent people being imprisoned, but that's a price worth paying?

'I've never been uncertain about the strength of utilitarianism in this regard,' Honderich replies. 'Other people have been much more uncertain. You, like me, seem to be a little tough-minded, but it can leave people breathless, because I think what you're suggesting is that it is okay to torture somebody to death, for example, in order to prevent an overwhelming tragedy, where the suffering to each of the people affected would be larger than the horror of torturing somebody to death.

'I'm rather of that mind myself. I can never really make out what is to be said against it. So I'm inclined to be with you, and be rather tough about it, but utilitarians have rarely been tough. They haven't been willing to defend their ground in the way that you're inclined to defend it for them. I suppose it's partly confusion. It might be that people mix up the correct judgement that it would be monstrous to torture somebody to death in order to prevent a million colds, with the much harder case that you're talking about, where, for example, it might be possible to prevent a thousand people from being tortured to death by torturing one person to death. In the latter case, maximization of satisfaction seems to be the rational course of action to take.'

Is it possible to go even further than this to say that one might be justified in torturing somebody to death, even if one knew that there was at least a possibility that they *didn't* have the information that one required, on the grounds that there was a good probability that they did, and that the gains to be had were such that it was imperative to get the information, for example, about a possible terrorist strike involving nuclear weapons?

'There are two things to be said about this,' Honderich replies. 'The first is that it has to be the case, as we have discussed, that the evil to be prevented is not only great, but it would be great to each of many people. The other thing is that it is easy here to slide into overlooking a certain fact. If it is a choice between a *certainty* of a horrific distress given a particular course of action, and a *probability* of avoiding some greater distress, where all people affected are so distressed, then you've got to remember that probabilities cannot weigh as much in argument as certainties.

'This came up with respect to the Iraq War, where it was really terrible to argue that we were justified in going to war, because there was some probability that Saddam would carry on as before. That was really monstrous, because it was excusing a course of action which was certain to cause many deaths on the basis of some unspecified probability that Saddam would behave in a certain way.'

But there is a counter-example here. Suppose that in the Second World War we knew that Hitler was creating a nuclear bomb, and there was probability x that he would be able to use it in anger. It doesn't seem in such a situation that it is obviously wrong to intervene.

'That's true,' Honderich agrees. 'If you adjust probabilities and possible harm, then you can get that kind of outcome. I'm perfectly prepared to admit that a course of action where it is certain that horrible distress will occur to some number of people might be justified if there is a high probability of overwhelming horror for a large number of people. I agree with that. But in the case of the Iraq war we were far from that situation.'

Honderich's general view is that punishment can only be justified in terms of a conception of the decent society. Why is this the case? Why can't we do it abstractly?

'The argument proceeds first of all by ditching the retribution theory – that's essential,' he responds. 'The retribution theory reduces to the unacceptable business that punishment is justified by satisfying grievance desires. So it follows that a consequentialist justification of punishment is the only possible justification. It seems to me then very clear that if you're justifying punishment by its effects, you've got to say what these effects are that justify it. This means that you have to lay out a conception of society which is such so that maintaining it or achieving it makes it worth putting people in jail and possibly executing them. I don't think there is any obscurity at all attaching to this idea.'

At first sight, this seems obvious. So why haven't philosophers been drawn to this view?

'Well, I think there's an interesting and large answer here to do with convention in philosophy and convention in thinking,' says Honderich. 'People have been subject to the illusion that something can be made out of the retribution theory. If you do think there is something in that, then of course you can avoid the challenging thought that you've got to say what the good is of punishment.'

Honderich works out the notion of the decent society in terms of a Principle of Humanity, which has six major components. The first and in some sense primary component, rooted in a fundamental human desire, is that people should have a decent length of life. The second is to do with material and bodily well-being, mainly the avoidance of pain, access to medicines, and also the minimal requirements for shelter, warmth and so on. The third is freedom and power in personal relationships. The fourth concerns respect and self-respect. The fifth has to do with the goods of relationships. The final component is the goods of culture, religion and education. Presumably, then, in terms of working out which specific punishments are justified in western societies, the main consideration has to be how well they stand up against these components of the Principle of Humanity?

'Yes, that's right,' says Honderich. 'I think, for example, it is more or less the case that most offences against property are such that their punishment in our society is wrong. People ought not to be in jail. Primarily this is because punishment of offences against property reinforces and protects a certain distribution of things. If you think that this distribution is vicious, which I certainly do, then you can't but think that this punishment is wrong. What you're going to do about it, isn't entirely clear. You take whatever rational steps you can in order to correct the distribution of means to well-being in such a way as to reduce the number of the badly off. If that means opening the gates of Wormwood Scrubs [prison], then you open the gates, and let the prisoners out. But it seems unlikely that it does.'

Honderich's position is that the system of punishment of any particular country underpins its rule of law, and therefore in a very real sense is the buttress of that country's social arrangements. It follows, therefore, that if these social arrangements violate the Principle of Humanity, one is morally amiss in supporting the system of punishment. But isn't there another possibility here: that one supports the system of punishment, even though it might secure bad social arrangements, for the pragmatic reason that it is precisely the most vulnerable in society, the people who are the victims of these bad social arrangements, who are most likely to be detrimentally affected by certain kinds of crime?

'I must admit to an immediate thrall of suspicion to that line of argument,' Honderich replies. 'I would suspect that the person who made this argument would be of conservative disposition. To say that we ought to go on punishing because punishment secures less offences against people who are already badly off seems to me to be open to deep suspicion. We know what punishment does. Whether or not it prevents some offences against people in lower social classes, what it mainly does is to reinforce and to carry forward a society that is fundamentally and terribly unjust. It maintains a property distribution, it maintains a distribution of means to well-being, which does not reduce the number of bad lives to the greatest possible extent.

'The other point to make is that if it were true that you could make a good argument to the effect that punishment reduces offences, which would be offences against people who are already badly off, so that they are better off than they'd otherwise be, then I've got nothing whatsoever to say about that punishment. My Principle of Humanity would commit me to persisting in certain kinds of punishment, if it were really true that it prevented offences which would bear on those who are already badly off. But I think on this question of fact, it is probably very unlikely that offences against property, for example, are these kinds of offences.'

There is an interesting issue here concerning those countries which measure up badly in terms of Honderich's Principle of Humanity, which has to do with whether or not these countries have the right to defend themselves. For example, if it is the case that Israel, given its current political and social arrangements, is contributing to the existence of bad lives, might it nevertheless still be the case that it is justified in defending itself against terrorism, even if on a certain view it is the kind of terrorism that might lead to social change and thereby to a reduction in the number of bad lives? To put this more starkly, do countries that are thoroughly bad still have the right to defend themselves?

'This actually brings to mind the American response to 9/11,' Honderich answers. 'In my book *After the Terror*, I make the point that you couldn't really ask America to do nothing; that it is

almost just a matter of human nature to defend oneself, and
that this issued in Afghanistan. So, in one sense, the question of
moral justification just doesn't come up. I think I'd say something
like that about the question you ask about bad societies or
countries. I can see how human nature might force them to
defend themselves.

'But supposing you were to give full details about whatever
it is that makes a particular country bad, maybe for example
it is a slave society, or a society based on the denigration of
one particular racial group. If, as a result, the rest of the world
decides to do something about this state of affairs, and you ask
the question whether or not this bad country has the right to
defend itself, well, I think you can answer the question by saying,
"Well, who cares if they have the right, it would be better if they
didn't".'

Nevertheless, it is possible that there is still an interesting
moral question here. Even in the situation just described, it seems
counter-intuitive to say that the bad country would be doing a
moral wrong by defending itself. The particular significance of
this line of thought is in relation to Palestinian terrorism and
Israel. Even if one thinks that Palestinian terrorism is justified
by the treatment of the Palestinians at the hands of Israel, then
if indeed it is just a matter of human nature to defend oneself
against attack, maybe an aggressive Israeli response to such
terrorism is justified, and if not, then at least understandable?

'I'm not going to grant you a large thing here,' Honderich
replies. 'If I do, I'll end up defending rape, because of course
rape is in line with human nature – well, it certainly isn't against
human nature. There can't be a large argument from human
nature to defence or attack in situations generally. The man
who defends himself against the person who intervenes to try
to stop him from violently raping a child, acts within his human

nature in defending himself. But it certainly doesn't justify him in defending himself in this way.'

Not even if his life is at stake?

'Well, that drifts over into the situation we were talking about earlier. It may well be that we all have a kind of invisible instinct of self-preservation, in which case the question of right or wrong doesn't really arise. I don't think that's a complete answer, but I think that it is the beginning of a complete answer.'

Honderich does not talk much about specific punishments in his book on punishment. But there is an interesting question here about whether capital punishment might be justified by the Principle of Humanity. Suppose, for example, that by executing Saddam Hussein, it makes the reconstruction of Iraq more easily accomplished, and therefore contributes to getting people out of their bad lives. Is this what we should do?

'I think I should reply by saying that just as there are very difficult factual questions about terrorism, mainly concerning the probability that it will work, there are also difficult factual questions about punishment,' Honderich answers. 'I don't feel amazingly well-informed about these things. But I'm not trying to bend any facts here. If it is established, or even made suitably persuasive, that capital punishment is called for by the Principle of Humanity then I have nothing against it.'

So Honderich doesn't have an emotional opposition to capital punishment?

'Yes, actually, I do have,' he admits. 'It's my inclination to think that it is against the Principle of Humanity. It creates a number of overwhelmingly bad lives – the poor bugger who is about to be given the lethal injection, his whole family, and all the rest. Equally, it contributes to a general tenor and character of society which gives rise to more bad lives. So I am against capital punishment. But that is consistent with granting a certain hypothetical, which is this: if it turns out that it has the effect of taking people out of bad lives, then I have nothing against capital punishment.'

Honderich ends his book on punishment with a fairly radical plea that we should seek to change the nature of our societies. If it turns out then that home-grown and foreign terrorism have a destabilizing effect which leads to the kinds of mass disobedience and protest that are likely to generate far-reaching social change should we offer our support to their activities?

'The answer to this is dead easy,' Honderich replies. 'If it is the case that supporting the activities of terrorists serves the end of far-reaching social change, which in turn serves the Principle of Humanity, then yes, of course we should support it.

'This is not a question to which my answer is embarrassing. If there is any virtue in the Principle of Humanity, then I'm persuaded that this is the position to which one is committed. We should shoot the Queen. Thus, with respect to the question of Palestine, and terrorism more generally, the difficult question isn't the morality of the actions, it is the factual question about whether terrorism will actually work.'

Suggested Reading

Humanity, Terrorism, Terrorist War: Palestine, 9–11, Iraq, 7–7 (Continuum)
Punishment: The Supposed Justifications Revisited (Pluto Press)
After the Terror (Edinburgh University Press)

5 Multiculturalism

Bhikhu Parekh

On my way to interview Lord Bhikhu Parekh, a fellow train passenger I was chatting to spotted my copy of Parekh's book *Rethinking Multiculturalism*. 'That's an interesting subject,' he said. 'It's a real time bomb.'

I was worried I was about to be on the receiving end of a diatribe about 'floods of immigrants' taking 'our jobs' and so forth. But it turned out this man definitely saw himself as an anti-racist and had been active in campaigning on this issue in the trade union movement. Nevertheless, he thought there was a problem of lack of integration, which he saw as being 'our' fault. For him, Britain's failure to assimilate its immigrants had created the 'problem' of multiculturalism.

'I think there's a tendency in many circles to say that multiculturalism is ghettoization,' said Parekh, when I told him this story. 'Each group lives the kind of life it wants to with nothing in common. This kind of ghettoization rules out a wider civil society where people interact. And if you don't have an interactive civil society, either the state disintegrates or it begins to run your society. In one case you have anarchy, in the other case you have a totalitarian society. Both are destructive.

'If this is what this man means, and I suspect it is, then he will say that it is precisely because he is anti-racist that he is against multiculturalism. The anti-racist makes two assumptions: the assumption of a common humanity; and also the assumption that racism is not only bad, but bad in such a way that we should not put up with it. We tolerate a lot of evils, so obviously we engage in trade-offs, but this is a non-negotiable absolute. Both these assumptions assume that there are shared values, which multiculturalism, understood in the ghettoization sense, seems to rule out.'

There is no one in Britain more qualified to discuss these issues than Parekh. He has combined academic excellence and a life in public service, most notably as a leading political theorist, and also as deputy, then acting, chair of the Commission for Racial Equality. The year 2000 was his *annus mirabilis*. The Runnymede Trust's Commission on the Future of Multi-Ethnic Britain, which he chaired, published its report; he published his important book, *Rethinking Multiculturalism*; and he entered the House of Lords as Baron Parekh of Kingston-upon-Hull. So when he claims that this ghettoized version of multiculturalism is false, you listen.

'I take multiculturalism to mean something different: that no culture has a monopoly on wisdom, no culture embodies all the great values, and that therefore each culture has a great deal to learn from others, through dialogue. What the dialogue does is to enable each culture to become conscious of its own assumptions, its own strengths and own weakness, to learn things from others. If this is what you mean by multiculturalism, in other words interactive multiculturalism, then I would say this is a very desirable thing. Not only is it very desirable, it is also one of the great common goods – that each of us should be able to liberate ourselves from narrow cultural parochialism, and open ourselves up to the influence of others.'

This is the essence of Parekh's multiculturalism, or to use a term he prefers, his pluralism. Many have thought that pluralism sounds suspiciously like relativism. But Parekh argues that there are clear differences.

'Relativism says values vary according to whatever unit of relativism you happen to take: from group to group, culture to culture, nation to nation, race to race, or even individual to individual. Because your values are ultimately socially, culturally or nationally derived, you are therefore trapped within them: you cannot get out.

'Pluralism is concerned with an entirely different perspective. It simply says, no single system of value captures all that is good or all that is worthwhile. It is therefore possible for different societies and different cultures to throw up different systems of value and to live by them. Even when we are agreed that there are values which are universally valid – liberty, equality, justice and so on – these values can be combined differently in different cultures.

'But one can go a little further. If you ask the pluralist why he holds his values, he would not give the relativist's answer – saying that they just are his values. He would give intersubjectively accessible and valid reasons which you can discuss. The pluralist is open to rational discussion, which a relativist is not. So a pluralist is open to influence, to absorption and dialogue in a way in which the relativist is not. For a relativist, no dialogue is possible because there is no shared language or vocabulary. For a pluralist it's not only possible, it's also desirable, because he is willing to learn from others.

'Here's a very simple example. In Singapore they recently passed a law which entitles parents who are over the age of 65 to demand that their children accommodate them in their houses. Something similar has also happened in Hong Kong. If you asked a Singaporean whether this is right, he might say something like: "These are our values, you have different values. You westerners are all individualists, you demand your own freedom. We don't live like that." He would talk like this and at first sight it does sound like a relativist argument. But if you probe him a little further, and say, look, you have Confucian values, yet in China they don't do this, and they don't do it in Malaysia either. Why are you doing this? He wouldn't just say these are our values, he would say that the Chinese and Malaysians are wrong; that these are great values, a part of a long tradition, and the Chinese and Malaysians have deserted the tradition. They should come back to it. He would also say "You westerners would benefit a great deal from our values because you have made a mess of your family by giving your children this kind of freedom." In other words, a pluralist does not give a relativist defence of his values, because he is in the business of saying, you can learn something from me.'

It is because of this commitment to pluralism that Parekh is critical of the idea that the 'problem' of living in a multicultural society can be solved by 'assimilation'.

'At the philosophical level, I have a problem with what is meant by assimilation. I'm from India, I've been here 40-odd years. What do I have to do to "assimilate"? Live like you, think like you? What does that actually mean? You live in different ways, depending on class, region, whether you're a man or woman and so on. How can I think like you? Don't you cherish our differences? I'm a different kind of person, with a different kind of background. I can't eat like you. Don't you like Indian cuisine? Don't you like my art? Assimilation is a very slippery notion, used very widely because it has some kind of intuitive plausibility. However, the moment you begin to deconstruct it, it either turns into a kind of moral totalitarianism, or it becomes too vacuous to have any meaning.

'It was interesting that when I was chairing the Runnymede

Commission, whenever we talked to conservatives who said they wanted people to assimilate and we asked them what they meant, they said they wanted people to respect the rule of law and democracy. But that's not wanting people to assimilate, it's wanting them to be good citizens.

'I have the same kind of difficulty with the idea of integration. What does that mean? That we can't disagree? Not that, we live in a democracy. That I can't disobey the laws of the land if it becomes necessary, as in the case of the demonstrations against Bush? No, we don't mean that either. Perhaps you want me to keep my garden clean just as you keep yours? Well, I can understand that, but then you don't require me to cultivate it in the same way that you do. So once you begin to try to spell out what integration means, it gets difficult.'

Because of Parekh's commitment to pluralism, he does not see any value in any kind of assimilation or integration that pressurises people to adopt a common culture, not least because the idea that there is a homogeneous common culture is a myth. The only kind of assimilation he approves of is one where everyone accepts certain key values, institutions and conventions.

'We happen to have certain institutions which bind us together and to which rightly or wrongly we have decided to subscribe. We have a parliamentary democracy, the rule of law and so on. These are public institutions, they hold us together and symbolize our society. What we ask is that people accept their legitimacy. Change them, fight with them, fine. But start by accepting that these are the legitimate institutions of authority.

'In this society, we also happen to have certain conventions. You don't walk around naked. You don't keep your garden hedge too tall, because if you do people will get upset and it will affect the value of the property next door.

'There are public institutions, norms of propriety, and certain basic values, procedural and substantive. That doesn't mean that you have to agree with them, but start by accepting them, because they are the ground rules. Then if you feel uncomfortable or have some objections, let's talk. You might say, look, you allow your girls to walk around in mini-skirts and I find this deeply offensive – I can see almost three-quarters of her body and I find this upsetting. So rather than talk about integration and assimilation in large and abstract terms, let us indicate what it is that we have in mind. I think it is right that there are things upon which we insist. But whether this is about integration, or cohesion, or whatever, I want to think in terms of concrete demands.'

This is the pluralist vision of a multicultural society which Parekh endorses. In a phrase used repeatedly in his commission's report, it conceives of society as a 'community of communities'. For many, it is no doubt an attractive prospect. But, as well as raising practical issues, it does challenge most of the key tenets of the secular liberal tradition to which many western democracies implicitly or explicitly belong.

Take the secular tradition. This demands that in the public realm 'the reasons you give must be of a secular nature. They must appeal to worldly interests and relate to what I can see, hear and feel.' This is why, for example, in France there is an ongoing debate about the rights of Muslim schoolgirls to wear the *hijab*. If the school is a public space and the public space is secular, then what is seen as a religious symbol has no place there. But Parekh believes that this kind of secularism is wrong.

'If you are a religious person who feels profoundly guided by certain absolute commitments, when you enter public life you are going to be drawing inspiration from those fundamental beliefs. If you tell these people: no appeal to God at all, no appeal to anything religious at all, you castrate them. You undermine not just the very basis of their beliefs but the very language in terms of which they think and talk. You are doing them an injustice. You are treating them unequally, because you have certain discursive privileges which you deny them. Given my commitment to multiculturalism, you are also denying yourself the opportunity of a dialogue with a different point of view, which for all you know may nurture certain sensibilities.'

The traditional secular liberal argument has been that in order to communicate in the public realm, we need to leave behind our culturally specific forms of language and, as Parekh puts it, 'transcend them all, and find one language that all can be expected to have, namely a secular language. My answer is that this is not an answer at all, because secular language is loaded.'

This is not the only problem Parekh has with liberalism. He cannot agree with it in its traditional form, for he sees it as not pluralist, but monist.

'Liberalism to me, as it has come down to us in the form of, say, John Stuart Mill, is a monistic doctrine. It says it is the only way of understanding human beings. They are, above all, individuals, who are rational, reflective, and must be able to revise their beliefs. However, this is a particular view, because in fact all of these premises can be questioned. Am I above all an individual? Certainly not for pre-modern Europeans and certainly not for Indians, Chinese and others who would say we are fundamentally embedded in structures of social relations. Gandhi, for example, who fascinates me, said he was committed to the individual but was not an individualist, because he would say that every man is born a debtor, with certain fundamental obligations, to the universe, to the civilization that made him possible, to his family. This is the starting point: not rights, but debts. This is not liberal. So my first difficulty with liberalism is that in the form it has come down to us, it claims to represent a set of fundamental truths about human life, and my response to that is that this is one way of looking at it; there are other ways.'

More recent liberals, such as John Rawls, have tried to define political liberalism in terms of procedural values for governing society rather than as a doctrine about substantive values which individuals inevitably disagree about. Parekh does not believe that this works either.

'My feeling is that every liberal is caught in a dilemma. If he is a pure proceduralist, then there is very little liberal about him. If on the other hand he gives it content, that content cannot be thin, it has to be fairly substantial for him to construct a theory. Once he does this, he is putting a closure on dialogue.

'Liberalism recognizes that differences exist, that on certain matters people have different beliefs. To accommodate these differences, liberals tolerate them, but publicly they don't take any notice of them. My multiculturalism looks at the whole thing very differently. I would say that if you want differences to exist and to be cherished, then you can't privatize all of them. Some have to be given public status. Why? There are three reasons.

'First, if diversity is privatized, and the public realm belongs to homogeneity, then homogeneity will be the publicly cherished value, because it is the only thing you publicly recognize. Anything that is private, personal or different is symbolically given less status.

'Second, if religion, for example, is privatized, then public resources will not be available to it. They will only be available to what is homogeneous.

'Third, even if you try to privatize differences, you will find that the public realm, which you want to make homogeneous, is homogeneous simply in the sense that somebody's difference is universalized.'

Parekh emphasizes that when he talks about a 'community of communities' he is talking about communities that are heterogeneous. Thus, people might talk about the Muslim community as if it were a homogenous entity, but in fact it is not. Nevertheless, the positive vision he puts forward is one where the community is in some sense privileged. The polity is arranged to respect communities and treat them as units worth engaging with, perhaps even more so than the individual. But isn't it possible that this kind of emphasis on community might lead to communities conceptualizing themselves in homogenous ways; that if society comes to think of itself as a community of communities, then this might actually exaggerate differences?

'Of course there is potentially a danger of an essentialism here, that you will freeze communities,' he replies. 'But I like to think that the specific way that I talk about communities avoids that danger. My argument is simply that in our society, and any society throughout history, although we are individuals, making individual choices, we are also members of different kinds of communities. Therefore, if you want to conceptualize society, it won't do simply to say, as Rawls does, that it is a society of individuals with a system of cooperation. That's only part of the truth. There are also communities, and I see myself as belonging to those communities. This is why we go to church or form part of local and ethnic communities and draw a certain inspiration from these things. I therefore ask myself, what is the best way to conceptualize our society? And my answer is that since individuals are embedded in communities, our society is a community both of individuals and of communities.'

Parekh does not believe, however, that communities are isolated from one another. 'No community can be frozen, because each community, and your commitment to it, will impact upon your membership of other communities. I see this as a fluid, interactive kind of social life, in which we belong to different communities and negotiate how they relate to each other. We are doing this all the time.'

One obvious problem with making pluralism the basis of public policy is that there are quite a lot of people who adhere to value systems which are absolutely not pluralist. And you don't have to look only to Islamic fundamentalists to find them. Roman Catholicism is certainly not pluralist, neither is Evangelical Christianity. Parekh himself acknowledges that this can be a barrier to the kind of dialogue he seeks.

'I remember when I was a young student in Bombay. We tried to organize a conference setting up a dialogue between different religions: Buddhists, Hindus, Catholics and so on. I wrote to the principal of St Xavier's College where I was a student, who wrote back two lines: "Since I believe that our religion is the only true one, an inter-religious convention is a contradiction in terms. You will therefore forgive me if I don't join you."

'How does one respond to that? Not everyone in our society is committed to pluralism, although society as a whole is. That is because we allow people to live by different values. This is what I think at one level is the strength of liberal society. A liberal society says you can be Catholic, Protestant, Muslim; you can have your own schools, forms of worship, magazines and so on. In that sense we do not just institutionalize but cherish plurality, in the hope that we will then talk to each other. We therefore have some kind of minimal commitment to pluralism.

'Now the question is, if there are bodies of thought which are absolutist or monist in my sense, what do you do with them? How do we live with the fundamentalist who says he doesn't care for liberal democracy?'

Parekh is aware of the problem but claims no easy solution. 'I don't want to give the impression that it is very easy to persuade people to see the multiplicity of truths or goodness.' He also concedes that he 'can't rationally convince the man who has taken an *ex cathedra* position, because it's not a rational position. He will allow reasoning only within the framework dictated by this absolutist commitment.'

Parekh accepts that 'liberal democracy provides one possible answer: we agree on certain minimum principles, we agree on certain minimum bodies and institutions, leaving us maximum space to live the way we want to. The dialogue resulting from our differences will inevitably shape the common culture and create a multiculturally constituted common culture.' But since this involves a privatization of much of culture and belief, and a lack of public recognition for differences, it is a position at odds with his pluralism. All that remains, therefore, is the hard path of dialogue and persuasion.

Arguably this is a rather optimistic prescription. But there may be alternatives. After all, pluralists are entitled to say simply that some value systems are just wrong.

'Could a pluralist say to someone, "This is unacceptable"? The answer is yes. A pluralist says that values can be combined differently, values need to be contextualized, different societies may choose to live by different values and so on. But he is not committed to saying that there are no universally shared values. Because he is committed to pluralism, he will reject all values that reject pluralism. If someone took the line that they had the only true or rational way to live, the pluralist would say that this was unacceptable. Because he is committed to the truth of pluralism, that values are inherently plural, that good is inherently diverse, someone who rejects that fundamental truth can be rejected by the pluralist. So pluralism has a built-in principle of universality.

'The other thing is that just because one is a pluralist that does not mean that there are no universal values, although they may take different forms. Take the Singaporean example. Here is a man who thinks that parents have certain rights. He would say there is a universal value: honour your parents. In my society, I honour it in one way, in your society, you honour it in another way, but if there is a society in which parents are not honoured at all, then that's not acceptable.'

It is possible to see why Parekh wants to avoid any trace of militancy. In conversation, it becomes obvious that pluralism is not just a theory to him. He genuinely lives according to its key tenets. He is openness, a desire for dialogue and a love of difference personified. When we talked at the House of Lords, two or three fellow peers greeted him, each one making a point of telling me what a wonderful man he is. He is in many ways the best advert for his own theory, living proof of the value of pluralism. But in a world of far more closed minds, is it wise or possible to construct a society along pluralist lines? I am not sure. But meeting Parkeh has made me think how good it would be if we could.

Suggested Reading

Rethinking Multiculturalism (Palgrave Macmillan)
The Future of Multi-Ethnic Britain (Profile Books)

Slavoj Žižek

'It's like discovering wild forms of sexuality after monogamy. All of a sudden they think, "My God you can do anything!" and they do all this crazy stuff.' The Slovenian philosopher Slavoj Žižek is talking disparagingly about philosophers from the Anglo-American 'analytic' tradition who 'switch sides' to Continental philosophy. After spending a couple of hours in Žižek's company, you can see he has a point.

Žižek is the antithesis of the cool, detached Oxbridge don. His writing and speech is bold, confident and contentious, illustrated vividly by countless anecdotes, jokes and references to Hollywood movies. The swagger of his prose is balanced by an ironic, self-deprecating modesty. After introducing himself, he offered me as a gift one of his books, which he signs 'with friendship', while at the same time dismissing it as a 'silly thing'. At one point he says, 'As I put it in I don't know which of my books, there are too many …', a sentiment he expresses more than once. He is certainly the only philosopher I have interviewed who begins by warning me that he 'gets confused' and that I should adopt an 'Orwellian' policy with regard to the accuracy of my transcription.

Žižek's speech is not so much confused as labyrinthine. He talks in an endless torrent, happy to stop if interrupted but equally content to continue indefinitely if not. There seems to be so much going on in his head that in order to get it all out he often has to leave various details unarticulated. 'And so on and so on' and 'Blah, blah, blah' are two of his most repeated phrases.

To say there is method in this madness is not quite right, for neither method nor madness is what Žižek is about. For sure, he does apply the methods of Lacanian psychoanalysis, which can make his work difficult for those not familiar with concepts like the *objet petit a*, the Real and the Symbolic Order. But his brilliance is not in how he interprets and applies Lacan, but in his frequent startling flashes of insight and the connections he makes between them.

Indeed, despite his firm basis in Lacanian psychoanlysis, Žižek hates being constrained by theoretical boundaries. 'I like to be surprised by unexpected encounters,' he tells me. 'I like this piece by piece approach – bricolage – you find something here and you find something there, and I don't care if they're officially ultra enemies of psychoanalysis.'

Hence he talks of his 'deep respect for Bernard Williams', his admiration for John Rawls, the 'miracle' of Saul Kripke ('for me analytic philosophy at its best'), his interest in the work of Donald Davidson and Jon Elster, even though the latter 'hates the guts of psychoanalysis and Lacan'.

What you don't get from Žižek is a programme. 'I openly say I don't have one. I am being honest here.' But when he has so much of interest to say about multiculturalism and the challenges of pluralistic societies, which questions almost every assumption of the usual debate, this hardly matters.

Žižek detects a tension in the thinking of multiculturalists. 'On the one hand, they elevate and idealize the other. But on the other hand, the moment you touch the topics of homosexuality, women's rights and so on, they are horrified at the other. I don't think they can really find the balance between these two. I think the only proper approach is to totally demystify the other. The best anti-racist book that I have read, a wonderful book, is Shepard Krech's *The Ecological Indian: Myth and History*. It makes the point that the Indians provoked worse catastrophes, shooting buffalos – they screwed the environment up. This to me is true anti-racism. You don't need to idealize the other. Honestly admit it – they are like us. We don't need this moralistic elevation of them.'

Žižek links this with the wider social phenomenon which he calls the 'logic of decaf coffee: the X deprived of its substance. Even in politics, you have with Colin Powell, warfare without causalities – decaf war. My point is that you also get decaf multiculturalism: you get the other, but magically deprived of its bad aspects.' In an irony he would be sure to appreciate, he says this while sipping a Diet Pepsi.

This ambiguous attitude to the culturally other is also manifest in the liberal notion of tolerance. 'I am more and more convinced that the very notion of tolerance secretly endorses precisely its opposite, a certain kind of intolerance. Tolerance means I shouldn't harass you. But for me, what the term harassment actually means is precisely "Don't come too near me with your intrusive presence." Harassment means I look at you and it's already aggression, sexual harassment and so on. It's this fear of the proximity of the other. For me, the fundamental contradiction of liberal tolerance – to put it almost in Hegelian terms – is that when they say "Let's tolerate each other" what in practical terms it usually means is "Let's stay away enough from each other."

'Those so-called multiculturalists who are against fundamentalism and for reason and tolerance, their hypocrisy is for me that the further away it is the better,' he continues. 'If you are native American, that's perfect, you can do whatever you want, it's part of your identity. But if you just imagine a WASP doing the same thing, saying "We want to assert our cultural identity" it would be proclaimed as proto-fascism. This is not just self-denigration, false respect for the other. It's that secretly you really privilege yourself. That is to say, you perceive others as constrained by their particular identity, whereas you are truly universal. Your very tolerance is your secret privileged, universal position. They get all the time caught in this structural inconsistency.'

Žižek's polemic is not wholly negative. His positive proposals, however, are likely to be unattractive to traditional liberals. 'Paradoxically as it may appear, what is needed is at the same time more universalism and more particularism. What I distrust with liberals is precisely this fear to assert their own identity.'

This is not a fear that Žižek feels. He recalls being at a conference in Malmo, Sweden, where people were speaking out against 'Eurocentric' conceptions of art. 'I exploded,' he says, apparently threatening to repeat the blast. 'I said, sorry, but for me, I'm not even Eurocentric, I'm Germanocentric. I claim that Italians write only operettas. I claim that there is something, Mozart, Beethoven, up to Schoenberg, which is unique. I'm claiming that's it. I think we should not be afraid of drawing these radical conclusions. I admire my good friend Alain Badiou, an anti-racist, who openly says in his new manuscript that only Europeans can think. Chinese cannot think. They cannot do philosophy. They have good political theory, they can do science, but they cannot do philosophy. They just use words.'

This flies in the face of conventional wisdom about liberal multiculturalism, but Žižek claims we need to 'fully assume the paradox that a true multiculturalism is strictly a Eurocentric phenomenon.' He rejects the claim that, for example, the tradition of tolerance in India provides good counter-evidence. 'European multiculturalism is not simply tolerance for others; of course you have that in India. It's something more. It's accepting your own tradition as radically contingent. And that I claim is something European.

'I even go a step further. I claim it's something Cartesian. It's interesting to read Descartes' *Discourse on Method*. The starting point is that he travelled around and saw people having different customs. And then he said that first he thought their customs were stupid but then he discovered that ours were stupid as well. This radical insight into the contingency of your own position is not just tolerance towards others. This is European.'

To use that tired old phrase, all of this is extremely politically incorrect. But Žižek argues that politically correct multiculturalism totally misses the point. 'I remember in my own country, which is supposed to be a symbol of ethnic struggle, how there were obscene, vulgar jokes about how each nation was identified in Yugoslavia with a certain characteristic. We Slovenes were misers, the Croats nationalists, the Bosnians sexually obsessed but stupid, Montenegrins lazy, Macedonians thieves. But I always claimed that these jokes were progressive. In what sense? First, for example, when I met my Montenegrin friends, we weren't exchanging insults. Each nation told jokes about itself. It was using obscenities to establish an informal solidarity. And my ultimate negative proof is that with the rise of true tensions in the early eighties, these jokes disappeared. This was the best signal that something was really wrong.

'This aspect is totally missing in my common daily experiences of meeting American, politically correct, tolerant friends. Some go so far that they are afraid to tell jokes, dirty jokes and so on, because, of course, a joke by definition is always in some way insulting someone. Did you know that they have now invented a kind of absolutely politically correct joke like, "What happens when a circle meets a triangle?" so nobody is insulted. I hate it.'

Whether it is authentically or inauthentically manifested, it is a mistake to think that 'the ultimate ethical horizon is that of respect for differences and recognition of differences'. It is an adherence to this tenet which for Žižek makes Derrida and Levinas 'in a fundamental sense' liberals, even though 'they would start shooting at me if I were to call them liberals. Beneath this big official animosity, there is a deeper solidarity between Derrida and Habermas. That is to say, for both of them the problem is recognition of the other, openness towards the other. It's just that they talk about different aspects. For Habermas, you need certain rules which guarantee tolerance, rules of democratic, open, free communication. For Derrida, you have to keep this more idiosyncratic openness. But the background is the same.

'But for me respect for differences as such cannot be the ultimate horizon. It has to be based on, I wouldn't say positive universal values, I would put it almost in more Marxist terms: struggling values, some sort of universal solidarity, or at least solidarity with universal intention. If I have respect for you and your difference it must be against the background of some presupposed notion that we share some dignity, participate in the same struggle potentially, or whatever. You cannot go, as they put it in reductionist terms, all the way down. Respect for difference cannot be the ultimate horizon. It doesn't work.'

What really concerns Žižek is that the focus on respect for the other, tolerance and so on, merely detracts attention from what is really important. 'Twenty or thirty years ago we were still asking questions about economy, democracy, political order and so on. 'Now, for example, take my big friend/enemy Judith Butler. Even if she officially likes to flirt sometimes with class and Marxism, she doesn't need that. She doesn't ask questions about the state and so on. It's simply questions about types of difference, right to marry and so on. Let's become aware that for these questions to be asked, other questions receded.

'The whole horizon should shift from these tolerance problems to – I'm very old-fashioned here – problems of universal struggle. Pragmatically, of course, I would be for tolerance and so on. I'm not crazy. I'm just saying that the paradox of these problems of tolerance is that if you try to solve them directly, you will not be able to.

'For me, the ultimate proof would be how by neglecting economic struggle, the left allowed the populist right in Western Europe to be the only considerable political force in Western Europe which directly addresses the working class. Let's cut the crap – for Haider and Le Pen, their main constituencies are the white working classes.'

This is why Žižek offers a qualified welcome for the success of Antonio Negri and Michael Hardt's *Empire*, even though 'I don't agree with my own blurb for it – you know, "The communist, manifesto for the twenty-first century". The publisher contacted me, I hadn't even read the book … But at least it refocused the topic a little bit on capitalism, the broader social dynamic, which was absent in the typical cultural studies of the nineties.'

Žižek's point is that, despite all the talk of gender and identity politics, the main divisions in society remain economic and social. 'In the United States, I claim, multiculturalism, and even feminism, quite often, I would say predominantly, has an upper-class attitude of dismissing the lower classes as primitive. In America, multiculturalists are always complaining, between the lines, about those stupid workers, those famous rednecks. It's basically a form of class consciousness.

'Take an upper-class enlightened guy. Different sexual orientation is the easiest to swallow. A well-spoken Indian is also easy to integrate. Social difference is the most difficult one, even though it's the most artificial one, the least natural.'

Žižek is no knee-jerk anti-capitalist, however. The only knee-jerk reaction Žižek suffers from is to knee-jerk reactions. He is quite cynical about the fledgling anti-globalization movement, which gained impetus when disparate groups came together at the World Social Forum meeting in Puerto Alegre, Brazil, in 2002.

'It's easy now in Puerto Alegre to sit together, conservative ecologists, Christians and whoever. My fear is that under their rhetoric of "we shouldn't play the game of power", they secretly don't even want power. They are in the hysterical position of enjoying resistance. Here I am, if you want, a Stalinist. I am not interested in resistance, I want power. I don't want to resist the enemy, I want to chop off his head, my God! That spirit is missing, I think.

'What annoys me is when some radicals, in order to avoid concrete analysis, take resort into what I cannot but call principled opportunism: being faithful to principles can in certain situations be the most opportunistic way. Because you're just faithful to principles, which means you don't need to do the really hard work.

'I'm here a pessimist. I claim we don't even know what is really going on today.'

This wasn't so much an interview with Žižek as an audience. But whereas with some people this would be irritating, with Žižek, his domination of the conversation feels like an act of generosity.

At one point, he clears up a possible confusion about his work with Lacanian psychoanalysis. 'I'm not a practising analyst,' he says. 'You know why not? After meeting me, let's imagine that you were to have psychological troubles, would you come to me?'

He has no desire or expectation that you will contradict the answer rhetorically demanded. But the fact that you would nonetheless willingly hear what he had to say about virtually any other subject testifies to his intellectual charm.

Suggested Reading

The Puppet and the Dwarf: The perverse core of Christianity (MIT Press)
On Belief (Routledge)
The Žižek Reader, ed., Wright and Wright (Blackwell)

7 Trust and Autonomy

Onora O'Neill

There are plenty of philosophers in Britain who have contributed to public intellectual life. Scour the various ethics committees, councils and commissions and you'll find people like Bernard Williams, Mary Warnock, Tom Baldwin, John Haldane, Peter Lipton and John Harris. Turn on the radio or look through the quality press and you'll find the likes of A. C. Grayling, Roger Scruton, Janet Radcliffe Richards, Mary Midgley and Anthony O'Hear. Their name is legion.

Many of these people are probably better known than Onora O'Neill, principal of Newnham College at Cambridge University. But look at her CV and you'll find a record of almost unparalleled achievement. For instance, there are currently very few philosophers in Parliament's House of Lords, and O'Neill is one of them (two others are Anthony Quinton and Mary Warnock.) Only three philosophers have given the prestigious annual BBC Reith lectures in their 54-year history and, you've guessed it, O'Neill is one of them. (Bertrand Russell gave the first in 1948 and John Searle delivered his in 1984.) And unlike some of her contemporaries, O'Neill's public work has not harmed her academic reputation. She is a highly respected philosopher whose work on ethics, practical rationality, and in particular Kant has been warmly received by her peers.

This almost perfect marriage of academic excellence and public engagement was reflected in the simultaneous publication of two new books in 2002. One, *A Question of Trust*, is the aforementioned Reith lectures. The other, *Autonomy and Trust in Bioethics*, is an academic work comprising the 2001 Gifford Lectures, a series as esteemed in the academic world as the Reiths are in the public sphere.

O'Neill moves between the two genres of public and academic writing apparently effortlessly. Reading the Reith lectures, you would have no idea you were dealing with a philosophical heavyweight, so unobtrusive is the philosophy. O'Neill has a simple explanation as to why the philosophy there needed to be so unassuming: 'Twenty-two minutes per lecture and an audience of a million people. What the philosophy can do is to give background structure but you can't show the bones too much.'

If there is a key to her ability to communicate to any constituency, from the radio listener to the senior academic, it lies in what she calls her 'secret view that you can discuss anything with anybody. I'm not particularly inclined to think that philosophy need issue only in arcane publications.'

At the same time she is not worried about those areas of her work that could never be of wider interest. 'I'd be the first to acknowledge that some of what I publish would be rebarbative to the world at large,' she admits. 'I publish plenty of things that probably fewer than fifty people read and of those only ten really chew it. I'm absolutely happy to go to meetings with very small audiences because it's something very specialized. I don't see a contradiction between having a specialism or groups of specialisms, and speaking to wider audiences. Some people might not enjoy that, but I have come to enjoy it.'

The topic which spans both her new books is that of trust, one she thinks 'philosophers should reclaim' from the sociologists.

'There is actually a huge amount of literature on trust from the last 30 years,' she explains, 'and I've only read a tiny fraction of it. But where I find the literature inadequate is that it interprets trust as a matter of attitude: do you have a trusting attitude or a suspicious attitude? And when you look at the well-known MORI polls that ask members of the public if they trust undertakers, estate agents or newspaper journalists they are of course asking about an attitude. It seems to me that by looking for attitudes you miss quite an interesting set of questions which are much more practical. What interested me was the practical point that all through life you have to place your trust or refuse your trust. We're constantly making judgements about whether to trust a particular agent or agency for a particular purpose in a particular matter and the judgement we make is, like other judgements, evidence-based. To highlight one's attitude is neither here nor there.

'I had a beautiful illustration of this in a point raised by a member of the audience in one of the Reith lectures who said that she didn't trust surgeons because her operation had been postponed. But the dreadful thing was she was having to wait another three or four weeks for her operation. If she really didn't trust surgeons she would have been delighted that the operation was postponed.

'What caught my eye was the question of what sort of information we need in order to judge whether to place or refuse trust. I think the interesting questions about trust are linked to our views about evidence and reasonable belief and above all testimony, and feed straight into epistemology and not into a study of social attitudes. That's why I think philosophers should reclaim the topic of trust.'

What O'Neill calls the epistemological issues surrounding trust are those concerning our justifications for placing or withholding trust. 'The epistemological link is that first of all you have to decide in a given situation whom you trust to do what. You have to specify both whom and what. For example, I trust the primary school teacher to teach my child to read. Why? I've read the Ofsted report which says that school does a good job teaching kids to read. But it doesn't tell me whether I should trust this teacher as a person. I might absolutely not trust her, I might think she's a terrible driver, I might think she is a scatty person who I certainly wouldn't trust to take my children to Paris by herself, or whatever. And I certainly wouldn't trust her to take my tonsils out. If you get specific in this way you can see that trust is always targeted. You trust a person for some purposes, but not for others. We might trust our immediate friends in a very broad and inclusive way, but even then there are likely to be certain areas where we say "I would trust so and so with my life, but as a matter of fact I wouldn't trust him to add up a column of figures because his arithmetic is a disaster." This sounds very commonsensical and down to earth because it is, I think.'

The issue of trust is important in areas of public policy, because of the rise of what O'Neill calls 'managerial and bureaucratic accountability'. Typically, the way this works is that 'management sets targets; those for whom the targets are set then perform; this is measured in certain simplified ways by performance indicators; and inadequate performance is sanctioned. This is supposedly a good managerial mode of holding to account. It's also highly disruptive and destructive of trust, because unfortunately the targets and performance indicators are very often subtly and sometimes greatly at variance with professional standards, so that people find themselves trying to meet two criteria simultaneously.'

The result is that we get hospitals focusing on cutting waiting times rather than providing good healthcare, or schools focusing on getting students through exams rather than providing a rounded education to prepare them for life. And with that we get the consequence that public trust in teachers and doctors diminishes.

This runs counter to good accountability, which in O'Neill's view 'provides the evidential basis for people to place their trust or refuse their trust'. But why has the accountability culture failed to build trust? 'I think the answer is that the culture of performance indicators and targets is really oblique to the judgements that people need to make. For instance, the way the performance indicator information reaches the public is often in the form of a league table. A league table enables a parent to judge of the locally available primary schools whether one is better or worse than another, very easily – anyone can read a ranking. But if you were to ask whether this school is better for this particular child or not, the league table doesn't help you, because (a) it's a comparative measure, (b) it's a measure with all the substantive information stripped out, and (c) so many artificial assumptions have had to be made to suggest that the performance indicator is a proper measure of quality. So no wonder we don't trust on the basis of league tables.'

Some might say that O'Neill is too concerned about the loss of trust. One line of argument is that trust requires personal relationships and in large modern societies so much of our interaction is anonymous or with strangers that the best we can hope for are guarantees and safeguards to act as surrogates for trust, not trust itself.

'Not all trust is based upon personal knowledge and I don't think it ever has been,' she replies. 'If we get the accountability right, and the way in which we provide information right, then people would be able to place their trust in certain institutions or not. I think that we greatly overestimate the role of personal relations in forming judgements about placing and refusing trust, partly, I suspect, because the literature has concentrated too much on the clinical encounter as the model. The clinical encounter happens to be an encounter where an individual meets an individual professional, or at least that was the traditional format. But that's never really been the way it has been when you had a correspondence with the tax inspector or when you checked on the telephone with the shop to see whether they can deliver such and such a commodity. Much trust is based upon an enormous web of beliefs that we hold with greater and lesser degrees of security, and very systematic, though often quite intuitively internalized ways of probing at certain points. That is why I say the topic is very close to the epistemology of testimony.'

There is also an objection that a healthy distrust is a good thing, a reflection of a desirable modern cynicism.

'What I'm arguing for could be called healthy trust or healthy mistrust. It is, after all, well-judged trust. Of course, in certain circumstances "don't put your trust in the snake oil merchant". If one wants to call that healthy mistrust, I don't mind. But the moment that thought becomes treacherous to us is when we imagine that there is something even better, that is refusing to trust anybody for anything. I think that's an illusion.

'Andrew Tucker of the Liberal Democrats argued in a pamphlet that in a mature polity there is no room and no need for trust. I know what he meant, which was that there is no need for a sort of childish trust, and I'd go along with that. But if he thinks there is no need for trust I think one should ask him how he proposes to decide what activities to engage in. If he said he would require a guarantee, well the fact is you can never get a complete guarantee. There's a sort of infinite regress problem here. Suppose I think, "I'm not going to take that on trust, I want a contract" and somebody asks me why I think the contract will be better. I say this lawyer is going to draw up the contract for me. But why do I trust the contract? Well I could get another lawyer to vet the contract. You can see the paranoia that develops out of the thought that you will have a complete regress in these matters.

'Of course there are ways of being more or less cautious, more or less systematic, about how you assemble evidence. But what you don't get is some magic way of leading your life where there are guarantees and proofs so that you never have to trust. Evidence is always imperfect, so you have to place your best bet this way or that way. I always feels this rather acutely when I have to buy a car. As I'm very inexpert, I do have to rely on somebody. But who, and why? Do I have a guarantee that they are perfectly objective? How do I know, for example, that the AA are independent and skilful? Is it just because they tell me that they are? So the idea of the trust-free life seems to me a really quite childish illusion.'

The major philosophical issue in *Autonomy and Bioethics*, which is also implicit in much of the Reith lectures, is the distinction between what O'Neill calls individual autonomy and principled autonomy. Individual autonomy is an idea which O'Neill believes has been 'very powerful in the late twentieth century' and she suggests that at least three of its roots may be 'certain early post-Second World War conceptions of the importance of individual choice, some versions of existentialism and the literature which debated the difference between the democratic personality and the authoritarian personality'.

'As I see it,' she explains, 'people who believe in individual autonomy generally share at least the following thoughts: it is a capacity or perhaps a property of individuals; it is something individuals can have more or less of – it's a gradated property of individuals; and also in consequence of that, you can speak of A as more autonomous than B.'

The puzzle for O'Neill is seeing why such a notion has been thought to be so important for ethics. 'I think the great problem is that if you took it as "mere sheer choice", which is a phrase I've used for the existentialist version, it is extremely difficult to see why it is ethically important. One might make a case for it being one of a number of important things, but many people have taken it to be absolutely crucial, and it isn't clear why it is.' The capacity to make choices, or even to make choices that we are able to reflect upon, does not seem sufficient to form the basis of our moral thinking.

However, the idea of individual autonomy is what lies behind the importance placed in medical ethics on informed consent procedures, and this is something which troubles O'Neill. 'People have very often taken it as a sort of mantra that if something receives informed consent it may be done. That's clearly false for lots of reasons, but there are terrible difficulties, particularly in the biomedical area, and I expect everywhere, when you ask the question of how informed informed consent must be. There are also terrible difficulties about how consent transfers from one proposition to another. Those are the two philosophical boulders that teach one to be just a little bit cautious about what informed consent can do for us.

'Let me give you a sense of some of the issues here as they apply in the field of biomedicine. If you think that individual autonomy, or in this context patient autonomy, is the key thing to protect, then you have to answer the question: how do you know that the patient is choosing autonomously? What you then find is that people give up on all their highfalutin conceptions of autonomy, and claim that we know that a choice is autonomous when a patient has signed the consent form. This has a great deal to do with protecting institutions against litigation. However, if you then get worried about the adequacy of the forms of consent we have traditionally used, you start to put the effort of accountability into inflating the demands for informed consent. You require that more information is given to the patient. But how do you know it has been given? Well, you have to have a box ticked to show that the information was forthcoming, or that counselling was offered, or that an information leaflet was given. The temptation then is to pile on the propositions to which the patient must consent. At the end of it, you have got something which in terms of current conceptions of accountability is greatly superior, because you've got this very much more explicit and detailed consent. But you also have to ask yourself, what does it all mean? What's really going on?

'I do think informed consent is important, but it is important, I suspect, not in a positive way, as a demonstration of individual autonomy. After all, the timid and cowering patient also signs the consent form. You can't say to him or her, your level of autonomy is really not up to it, could you please up it a bit so that you give proper consent!'

O'Neill, however, is not optimistic that these kinds of philosophical reflections are likely to result in changes to the way in which consent is handled. 'I'm always fairly modest about what I think philosophy can do in these matters,' she says. 'I think there is some helpfulness in being very familiar with the background arguments in political philosophy and also not being over-deferential to the arguments, because you know how much they presuppose and what they assume. I would guess in this area the only advantage philosophers have is that they are perhaps a bit more likely to know that this isn't the first time people have had terrible debates about consent, and they are less likely perhaps to appeal to some mantra of informed consent and think that settles the matter.'

A far better notion of autonomy than this idea of individual autonomy, O'Neill believes, is the Kantian conception of principled autonomy. 'Kant of course thinks that individuals have the ability to choose, but he happens to call that spontaneity, not autonomy. He calls a choice autonomous only if it has a distinctive structure, so that the mere fact that it is my choice or even that I reflected on it and chose it, won't make it autonomous.'

Autonomy – or self-legislation to give the term its literal etymological meaning – is not then, for Kant, merely about the self – the individual – making rules for itself. 'For Kant, of course, there is a sense in which the self self-legislates, but the self also adopts all sorts of appalling maxims. So you might adopt the maxim of self-love and in the modern sense of the term that would be self-legislation. What Kant is interested in is the quality of the legislation bit of it.

'What is very interesting is that though people use this metaphor of self-legislation for the etymological modern counterpart of autonomy, they actually completely drop consideration of the legislation or the *nomos* part of it – law or principle. Kant does not. As I read him, his take is that there are many sorts of principles which are highly derivative, for example, from my own desires, from certain ideologies, from the power of church or state or whatever it might be. All of these in his view are legislation but they're legislation that assumes something other: heteronomy.'

Heteronomy is legislation by an other: it is other- (hetero) legislation (nomos) as opposed to self- (auto) legislation. 'From the point of view of ethical justification,' continues O'Neill, 'in heteronymous principles in that way, you've then got a completely arbitrary premise, because it's always going to be a version of the argument from authority, with a lot of different ideas about what's an authority – my desires, the king or the parish priest, or whatever.

'Whatever sense Kant gives to autonomy it has to contrast with heteronomy. I think that his thought is simply the negative counterpart: an autonomous principle is a principle that is not derived from some arbitrary, ungrounded authority – church, state, king, own desires, whatever. It's not heteronymous. But it is nevertheless a principle. It isn't, as he puts it in many passages, something completely lawless, for what it is to be a principle or law is to be a principle that could be followed by any number of agents. So Kantian autonomy ends up being defined in terms of acting on a principle because it has, as he puts it in many passages, the form of law. Acting on a principle not because of who commands it but because of its structure.'

The question then arises as to whether, as O'Neill puts it, such a principle 'cuts any ice', or actually tells us anything about what we should do. 'My contention would be, though it's a long story, that it at least eliminates those principles which could not be universally adopted, because if they were universally adopted, then if some people acted on them successfully, at least some others would not even be able to adopt them. For example, I can as an individual want to be a slave master but I cannot universalize slave-mastery, because in a world where that happened at least some people would be enslaved and where some people are enslaved, then you would have the problem that those people couldn't themselves even set about being slave masters.'

O'Neill's full justification for this textual reading of Kant is detailed and would involve reference to those 'rebarbative' academic papers mentioned earlier. One short and sharp point worth making in defence of her reading is that 'it solves the problem of why it is thought autonomy is connected to morality in Kant. The answer is not that his sense of morality is warped and outlandish, but it is that his conception of autonomy is quite different from the late-twentieth-century conception.'

O'Neill admits that she considered adopting a different term to distinguish this Kantian notion of autonomy from ideas which emphasize the primacy of individual choice. However, in the end she decided to keep the term. 'I wanted to show how its curious pedigree had survived, and I've read enough of the contemporary literature on autonomy to see that it is one of the big posh words to use, and people think that in doing so they're getting the whole Kantian tradition. So that's one of the reasons I kept it. But the other reason is that I wanted to show how there is a way of thinking of autonomy which is not individualistic; that it can be a principle for all, not because everyone in fact adopts it, but because it has that capacity, that structure – like that we will all reject slavery. My view is that the word has slid far enough into popular currency at present that the default meaning is the individual meaning. But it is interesting to find, for example, that Mill nowhere thinks he can use the word autonomy to mean individuality, or character, or independence of choice, or any of these various phrases he uses. That kind of usage of the term is a twentieth-century thing.'

For O'Neill, this idea of principled autonomy has implications for wider issues to do with trust. 'Some of the things that you get out of a consideration of principled autonomy are the rejection of coercion and the rejection of deception. Both these are absolutely necessary for creating a good basis of evidence for people to judge where to place and refuse trust. I have no illusions that we will end up in a world in which it is feasible to trust only the trustworthy and to mistrust only the untrustworthy. However, the relevant thing for enabling us to make decisions about trusting is that we build up an evidence-base that others are not deceiving us and that they are not coercing us.

'What is also very interesting is what we do when we think that we're often being misled. We don't in fact say "I don't trust", because the evidence-base tends to be too confused for that. We find ourselves in a sort of suspended animation, neither believing nor disbelieving. Listen to intelligent people retelling gossip from newspapers: they will put in caveats, and will say, "Well, of course, it may not be true" or "I don't know how much evidence there is for it," and then they go on retelling it, but they tell it as they might tell a myth, they're viewing it as gossip all the time, which I think is quite a dangerous situation.'

O'Neill says she suspects that she has been an 'awful trespasser', meaning that she has not been shy of straying into disciplines other than philosophy. For those inspired to follow her example, the secret of successful trespassing may be quite simple: lunch.

'Long before I came to Cambridge where that is institutionalized through the medium of the college, I've always made a point of lunching with people who weren't necessarily in my own discipline. I've always found that helpful,' she says, before adding, 'by which I don't mean I don't talk to philosophers.' Whether talking with philosophers or non-philosophers, addressing the public or the academy, Onora O'Neill is living proof that there is no need for either/or. But to do both as well as she does almost certainly is beyond the reach of most of us – including her peers.

Suggested Reading

Autonomy and Trust in Bioethics (Cambridge University Press)
A Question of Trust (Cambridge University Press)

A. C. Grayling

A. C. Grayling is that rare beast: a famous academic philosopher. In Britain, he is arguably the best-known of the public philosophers. His steady output of columns, reviews and books has become a torrent in recent years. His latest tome, *The Mystery of Things*, is his fifth substantive book aimed at a general readership in as many years.

Confirmation of Grayling's minor celebrity came when he was the victim of a recent lampooning by the satirical magazine *Private Eye*, which claimed he had a tendency to repeat himself. But some things merit repetition. Grayling, professor of philosophy at the University of London's Birkbeck College, is a passionate advocate of philosophy and the value of rationality, and to be a champion of reason requires the repeated removal of heads from the hydra of irrationality.

Grayling straddles the worlds of academic philosophy and public discourse with apparent ease, at home in both. In his subterranean London office, which resembles a book depository more than a study, he explains that this is because, for him, there is little to separate them. 'My bottom line is that philosophy, for all of its apparent abstraction and technicality, is really just a membrane away from ordinary, everyday practical concerns.

'Absolutely everybody, to some extent, has got a philosophical outlook,' he says. 'They have committed themselves to certain philosophical standpoints, even if they don't themselves realize it or put that name to it.

'During the course of history, there have been those who have paused and thought a bit about the assumptions that we are making and the beliefs that we're committed to. We've noticed that we believe things, we take ourselves to know things, that we're certain about particular things, that we think this is the way the world is, that we grasp the truth. Then we start having second thoughts: what is knowledge? What is truth? What is it to know something? What are the correct means of getting knowledge? How can we communicate with each other about these things? We seem to be taking more steps away from those original concerns, but it seems to me that the distance between them is always very short, and therefore the sparks that fly in that debate will illuminate what is happening in your ordinary experience.

'Philosophy, in its history, is a great repository of discussions about things that matter and of examples of people trying to think their way through dilemmas. It's up to philosophers, who know about these things, who have had the opportunity and the privilege of studying them and the time to read them, to try to make them accessible without making them simplistic.'

The plausibility of this argument diminishes when one considers the abstruse nature of much contemporary academic philosophy. Yet Grayling maintains that even here, the gap between the interests of the intelligent, enquiring person in the street and those of the academic philosopher is not all that large.

'It's inevitable that academic philosophy is going to make a lot of use of jargon, and it's going to trade a lot on the understanding that you expect your readers to have,' he says, by way of explaining the trouble people have seeing the point of such philosophizing. 'Philosophy has become so jargon-laden and so technical that in order to gain access to it you've got to go through a process of study, of induction. It's a bit like having to train for the priesthood.

'But at the same time, even those technical fields are only a couple of steps away from applying to our thinking about ourselves and the world. What one therefore ought to do is to try to show people that there are philosophical ideas and techniques which are of genuine value for the public debate about things that matter to us, if it were possible to export them from the technical discussion in philosophy.

'I'll give you an example. Think about our attitude towards mental health, to the mind, to treatment of mental disturbance. Immediately a whole range of questions crop up: is there such a thing as insanity, or is that just a way of being human that is different from the convenient norms of the rest of society? A researcher asks what is going on, whether this is a disturbance in the electrochemistry of the brain or something purely in the psychology; something in the software or the hardware. If it's the hardware, will we be able to solve all these problems by means of drugs? If it's somehow in the running of the programme, then if people have maladaptive responses to the world, would you be able to aid them by helping them to better responses to the world? You see, all those questions prompt philosophical debates one could have about the nature of the mind and its relation to the body, and how we classify and think about these things.

'Or, to give another example, look at the arguments we have about education. We have had a huge problem for nearly 50 years in this country about how to organize an educational system. Are we educating people or are we training them? Are we training them to be foot soldiers on the economic battlefield or do you want to teach them to think for themselves and find out information for themselves? Is education a process of drawing out natural abilities and talents, or is it trying to give something to people that they didn't previously have? So all sorts of questions arise – about human nature, about the purpose of education, about what it is to learn something, and about the value systems we operate by.

'All these things involve philosophical questions. One could take lots and lots of other examples, and in every case you'll find that there are philosophical issues there.'

Isn't it the case, though, that when people talk up the way that philosophy might contribute to public understanding, they're actually thinking of the work of the big names – Hume and Descartes, for instance, or in recent years one of the major theses of Rawls or Nozick? Very rarely is anybody going to say something like 'Well, here your ideas could be illuminated by something Christopher Peacocke wrote in a paper in *Mind* in 1973.' As a matter of fact, then, isn't the vast majority of academic philosophy of little use to the educated public?

'It might look that way, but actually it's more complicated than that,' Grayling replies. 'Hume and Descartes are interesting, because they were writing for the educated public, not for other academics. They just took it, and their readers took it as well, that people who were thoughtful and wanted to be informed needed to read this stuff. In the seventeenth and eighteenth centuries, philosophy really mattered. Epistemology really mattered because people needed to know what kind of enquiry was going to get genuine results and what kind of enquiry was just going to lead to astrology and alchemy and so forth. We're at the far end of that process, and we've sort of got it right, mostly, if you think of the sciences, and so epistemology seems to be "only academic" but then it certainly was not.

'But to go back to Peacocke and some paper in *Mind*. If you're working in robotics, let's say, or in computing science, you might be very interested to know something about spatial reasoning, let's say. Or if you were working on programmes to try to effect translations between languages in ways that were genuinely sensitive to semantic nuances in the host language, then you might want to know something about the nature of reference and predication, and you might actually profit from technical discussions of these things, so that you could build them into something practical.

'I've always thought that there are likely to be concrete applications for ideas about perception, spatial awareness, that kind of thing. Indeed, if you look at twentieth-century cognitive science, you'll see that it was heavily influenced by linguistics, logic and the philosophy of mind – it's a perfect example of how people working in very abstract areas of philosophy can find that their work has an impact upon and influences people working in other fields.'

Sometimes then the relevance of technical philosophy will be for other technical disciplines. However, on other occasions, and this is where Grayling shines, the contribution philosophy makes is to a more general need to understand our place in the world. Here, Grayling believes the main contribution philosophy makes is to provide resources to help each individual's own thinking.

'The reason I often write short essays is that if you write a long one you are generally offering an argument with a conclusion – this is what I think, and I hope you agree with me. If you write something short, that just reminds people of pointers in the debate. It's like a hint or a nudge: it either pushes people to find out more or it gives them a little grain of something which serves as the germ of a thought for them. I think that if you do it well enough you can achieve the *multum in parvo*, the much in little. You can get ideas and points across in a concise, accessible, attractive format, and get people thinking.'

Grayling is a big fan of the essay, which he now sees as living on in the form of magazine and newspaper articles.

'The beauty of the essay is that it is conversation in prose. It's completely general in what it can cover. To be a reader of the essay is to get a tremendous general education. In the past, there wasn't so much television and so on, so people used to read essays, and they wanted something substantial to get their teeth into. So they would get something like the *Edinburgh Quarterly*, once a quarter, and it would take them the whole quarter to get through some pretty substantial essays in it. We can't quite do this now. Everything has become compressed because it's a much more hurried world. But I still think that if you employ sufficient mastery you can get people thinking. The really crucial thing is that you want people to look up from the page, and say "Oh, that's interesting," or "I don't agree with that," or "I have to find out more about that," or "Who is this person, what's his name, I think I'll go to read him." Just think, if you are read by ten thousand people on a Saturday, and five people go to the library or on to the Internet as a result, then that's actually an achievement isn't it? You've actually done something, you've justified your existence.'

Is this kind of thing likely to be considered proper philosophy, though? It is not unlikely that professional philosophers would look down upon writing that doesn't attempt to cover all the bases, or to show that something follows logically from something else.

'I think that was true for quite a long time after the Second World War,' Grayling agrees. 'But it certainly wouldn't have been thought before then. Russell, for example, Santayana, Moore and various other people, accommodated themselves to their readerships. Russell wrote many, many popular books. Admittedly, they were potboilers and they were for making money, but when he was writing about marriage and morals, he didn't write using the idiom of *Principia Mathematica*.

'Even today, I think there is reason for hope. Here at Birkbeck, for example, we recognize that there is no point in thinking you're going to persuade people that philosophy is interesting, valuable and life-changing just by giving them a couple of pages of the *Principia* to read. That's not going to work. You've got to say to them, this is where this adventure begins, and it begins because we're not that far away from all the things that really matter. And if you look around, there are people such as Simon Blackburn and Roger Scruton who are doing a wonderful job communicating more widely. It does seem that it is getting more respectable to do it.'

In order to bring philosophy to the public successfully, however, it does require that people have a thorough grounding in the subject. 'Anybody who is serious about philosophy should work hard at getting a very deep understanding of some special field – that's your anchor in philosophy. Otherwise you are just floating on the surface all the time.' But Grayling also insists that 'philosophy is a much bigger thing than academic philosophy'. The professionalization of philosophy has tended to occlude this fact. It restricts what is legitimately seen as philosophy, by making it the preserve of a professional few, and at the same time it makes it possible to be a professional philosopher while not being a true philosopher at all.

'I think a distinction needs to be drawn between a philosopher and a person who teaches, because not all teachers of philosophy are philosophers,' he explains. 'To claim to be one is an act of temerity really. It's an accolade that somebody else might give you if you merit it. To succeed in being a philosopher is to think justly, deeply, truly and fruitfully about things, and try to live accordingly. There are plenty of genuine philosophers, people who live philosophically and thoughtfully, who have never studied philosophy, never taught it, never been near a university; and there are plenty of people with a profound capacity for philosophical insight who are busy writing novels, poetry, composing music, making films or acting in them.'

Obviously, there is a lot to be said in favour of greater philosophical input into public discourse. However, it is also the case that philosophers are not always terribly impressive with what they come up with when they are asked to comment on the affairs of the day.

'I completely take this point,' says Grayling. 'The thing is that when there is some great moral panic in society, what tends to happen is that the news people trot out a bishop or two for their comments, and it's entirely predictable what line they're going to take. But of course they are not the only people who think about such things, there are also dozens and dozens of philosophers who might well very usefully be asked about them.

'If they do get asked to comment, philosophers have to avoid making the mistake of thinking that they're in a lecture hall, or in a seminar, or to think that they're talking to their professional colleagues, and therefore they've got to be absolutely careful about every word they choose. They've got to think about how to parlay their understanding or viewpoint in a way which is not naïve in failing to take the practicalities into account, and which does address itself to the interested and intelligent general public. This is just a matter of technique.

'When it comes to political things, things about the Iraq war, for example, then emotions are engaged as well, and people have political views. This does make a difference to the kinds of things that people say, and it can make philosophers seem like the next guy on the bus, or a cab driver. You're right that if you haven't quite mastered the knack – and it's a very difficult one to master for anybody – of making a point well in a very short space of time, then you are going to sound glib and superficial. But then it's not only philosophers who sound glib and superficial.'

If Grayling faces a philosophical problem in fulfilling his role as a champion of rationality, it is that the nature of rationality itself is a disputed area of philosophy. How can he advocate rationality as a value in public life when philosophers don't agree on what rationality is?

'The concepts of reason and rationality have fuzzy boundaries,' he explains. 'The philosophical debates about what's reasonable or rational tend to be about trying to find the line within the fuzz. But a focal case of rationality is where people proportion their commitments or beliefs to the evidence or the reasons they have for holding those beliefs, where their beliefs and the actions that they take are responsibly, maturely and sensibly reached. By that I mean that somebody could make a really cogent case that anybody else, who shared this responsible sense of trying to do things in ways that really did match the evidence, would recognize as good reasons for believing or acting that way. This is a good, clear sense of what it means to be rational.

'Now we generalize this to society as a whole, to religious belief, to our ethical commitments and to our political actions, and say: let's try to live reasonably, on the basis of good reasons. I mean by that not only what I've just said about trying to act and think maturely and respecting the evidence, but also bearing in mind what it excludes, namely prejudice, supposed instinct, supposed intuition, ancient scriptures, and all the other things that people lazily use as the basis of the premises for the arguments they run. That's what it is to try to be rational in society.'

Grayling says that he becomes 'heated' when he sees fellow academics trying to undermine this straightforward sense of rationality and its value, singling out 'John Gray and his coterie' who advocate 'anti-liberal values, anti the idea of human rights, anti the idea of human values, anti the idea of rationality, and so on. That's a kind of pose, something to do. Let's combat the orthodoxy, it's great to attack the orthodoxy, to get a debate going, to kick up the dust. It seems to me utterly irresponsible, because people live and die, and kill, on the basis of their beliefs, and this is not a matter for messing around with.'

Equally, he defends Enlightenment values against those who claim, like Adorno and Horkheimer, that they led inevitably to the terror of the French Revolution and even Auschwitz. 'The fact is that the Enlightenment always casts a shadow. Look at the counter-Enlightenment in the eighteenth century, what people were trying to assert against those principles. There is always a battle to be fought with people who reject those values. But those values seem to me a great achievement. It's an achievement to have liberated gays and women from the oppressive prejudices that people had in the past. This is an outcome of trying to think reasonably and sensibly about things. So reason matters, and the sort of values that it gives rise to really matter.'

Grayling is probably best known for his strong anti-religious views. He is of the opinion that the religious are irrational, pure and simple. 'They are certainly irrational about their choice of premises. There's a certain kind of psychopath who reasons with ferocious logic from terribly distorted premises, and of course you end up with a serial killer or something as a result. That's a familiar enough phenomenon, and that seems to me to parallel the case of religion.

'The reason people accept the premises of religion has almost everything to do either with how they're brought up, or their emotional state: these are emotional choices they have made. I'm impressed by the arguments of people like Antonio Damasio who say that good reasoning is tinged with emotion. Unemotional thinking is in fact as bad as over-emotional thinking. So, I'm not against emotion. But to choose your premises purely on the basis of emotion – on the basis of a need, a fear, or how you were brought up – that's the irrationality.'

Grayling sees the mistake of the religious to be essentially metaphysical. There is nothing distinctly religious, he argues, about what religious people call the spiritual – 'our feelings sometimes of oneness with the universe, our sense of the numinous, our sense of things being soaked through with significance or value, our appreciation of beauty, our need for friendship and for love' – or the ethical.

That leaves only a certain metaphysical view peculiar to religion, that 'the universe is such that it contains supernatural agencies of a certain kind. Ask yourself the question: on what possible basis could it be rational to think that there are any supernatural beings? The argument for saying that there is a god as conceived in one or another revealed religion is as good or bad as the argument for saying there are fairies at the bottom of the garden.'

The analogy is not frivolous or condescending, but extremely pertinent. 'More people believed more vividly and passionately in the existence in fairies up until the late nineteenth century than they did in the existence of God. Fairies did more things than God ever did. They had to be propitiated. God didn't come and pinch your shoelaces, the fairies used to do it.' The question implied here is, if we can see how crazy it is to believe in fairies, which until recently most people did, why can't we also see it is crazy to believe in other supernatural beings? It's such lousy metaphysics that it seems very hard to imagine how anyone who cleared the decks of all his presuppositions and prejudices could believe it. 'I think that if it weren't the case that in this country over 80 per cent of church schools are primary schools, and if you went to a mature adult who had never thought about religion before, and you told him the stories and asked him to believe them, he would laugh at you because they are literally ludicrous.'

Not just ludicrous, but dangerous. 'Religion has been such a force of harm in human history. Human beings have groaned under the weight of oppression, limitation and restriction as a result of these beliefs. I ask people to look at history and ask the following question: if you allow a religious movement to become dominant in a society, to actually get its hands on the levers of power, what stops them from becoming the Taliban? Nothing. In the past, in the history of the Christian churches over the last two thousand years, up until the point when they lost intellectual credibility and power, in the seventeenth century and subsequently, that's exactly what they did: they burned people at the stake for disagreeing with them. I am filled with pity when I think of what people suffered all their lives long as a result of what religion did to them. I look around the world today and see that the majority of conflicts in the world have their roots in religious passions. What are they arguing over? Fairies. It so dismays me that I could weep when I think about it. Religion is a cancerous tumour in the history of mankind.'

Grayling's militant form of atheism can put off many who might otherwise find common cause with his advocacy of reason. But, as his earlier remarks about the role of the essay show, his campaign is not primarily about rallying around a position or a camp but stimulating public debate so that the rational comes to occupy more and more of it. You don't need to agree with Grayling about all his views to think that a worthwhile goal. You've just got to be reasonable.

Suggested Reading

The Form of Things (Weidenfeld & Nicolson)
The Mystery of Things (Weidenfeld & Nicolson)
What is Good (Weidenfeld & Nicolson)

9   Making Babies

Mary Warnock

We all know we shouldn't judge a book by its cover. But with Mary Warnock a further caution is needed: do not judge an author's interests by her book titles.

The last time I spoke to Warnock (see *What Philosophers Think,* pp. 152–160) it was about her anthology on women philosophers and it transpired that she had little interest in the subject at all. She happily admitted, unlike countless authors who do the same, that she wrote it because she was asked to and she needed the money. Now she has a new book out: *Making Babies: Is There a Right to Have Children?* But despite the question of the sub-title, she would rather people didn't talk in terms of rights at all.

The book's main theme – the ethics of reproductive technologies – has been a mainstay of Warnock's work for decades. She chaired the Committee of Inquiry into Human Fertilization and Embryology, which was set up after the birth of the world's first 'test-tube baby' in 1978. The advent of in vitro fertilization had caught professional medical ethics napping and the committee was charged to look into what regulations should govern these new techniques and the moral status of the embryos they created. Since then, reproductive medicine has continued to forge ahead and Warnock has remained pre-eminent among those dealing with its ethical implications.

Warnock has generally welcomed advances in reproductive technology, recommending clear regulations that, in many people's view, draw a sensible line between the permissible and the unethical. Nevertheless, she has become increasingly concerned about an unwanted side-effect of the availability of these techniques.

'I think there is an increasing tendency for people to demand medical or remedial treatment as if it were a right,' she explains. 'People are prone to think that they can have whatever they want as a matter of right, and having a child is sometimes what they overwhelmingly want. This really does change the relation, in this case, between doctor or clinic and patient. And then there is a great threat of litigation for all providers of services if the service doesn't work. There really seems to me to be no justification whatsoever for bringing in the concept of rights in this case.'

Warnock believes the root of the problem is a failure to understand the relationship between rights and duties. 'I do not think that it makes sense to say that you have a right unless someone has a duty to make sure you get what you claim. For example, if you have a right of way over my property then it's my duty to ensure that you've got a free passage. If somebody has a right then he is claiming someone else has a duty to supply him with what he is claiming. But this is not always possible and if it isn't possible – well, I'm not sure it makes sense to talk about the right to have a child, for example.

'This led me to draw the distinction between the right to have someone try to help one have a child and the right to have the child, because there are limits beyond which the doctor or the clinic cannot be said to have a duty.'

Warnock has some sympathy with the view of the great utilitarian philosopher Jeremy Bentham that ultimately rights are not fundamental, but rather are always an expression of something that can be explained in more fundamental terms.

'I go along with Bentham in the sense that if there can be adduced no law, no principle, then to talk about a right is nonsense on stilts,' she explains. 'I think that the random claiming of rights all over the place is really a moral statement that people ought not to suffer the things that they do suffer. So it's the statement of a moral principle that it's generally morally wrong that people should be allowed to starve, for example. But even then, the question arises, who is responsible? Is it my duty, our duty, or society's duty to ensure that people don't suffer from poverty in central Africa or wherever? When people talk about countries that have a bad human rights record, presumably they mean that the government of that country is failing in their duty to the people who belong to that country. But it's very dangerous then to say that we all have this duty because that's what leads to people saying we ought to invade Afghanistan or whatever it is.

'I mean there's such a muddle in what's going on in Washington. It's partly that the people of Iraq are supposed to be suffering, their human rights are being neglected. It's partly, of course, that the Americans feel themselves that their right to live in security and not be threatened has been overthrown and that the terrorists, whoever they may be, have neglected Americans' rights to live peacefully, and that's why they have to be taught a lesson, so to speak. I find the thinking behind this warmongering talk very confused but also very frightening.

'I'm very unclear as to what would nowadays count as a just war. I suppose a war motivated by the threat of invasion would count. But I can't see that the fact that some human beings are being badly treated somewhere or other could possibly be a justification for war unless it became clear that everyone in the world thought this was the only thing to do. This is why the thought of a war against Iraq without the United Nations seems to me to be absolutely monstrous.'

Less globally, Warnock is concerned that the mentality of rights is having a damaging effect on the relationship between doctor and patient, and more generally on how we view life's vicissitudes. It encourages us to think about things as being owed to us which previously we would have been grateful for or seen as opportunities.

'You see people now sue or threaten to sue their school for not having taught them properly,' says Warnock, by way of example. 'We used to think we were very grateful for the education we got, or else that it was lousy education and we wish it had been better. But the idea that someone had a positive legal duty to supply one with what one wanted seems to me very peculiar. Part of what it is, I think, is a confusion between what you are entitled to as of law and what you very much want. It's very easy to confuse those two things.

'It enters into all kinds of areas, such as personal relationships. People say things such as they have a right to be told the truth. Well you *want* to be told the truth but who gave you the *right* to be told the truth? It seems to me that the language is aggressive, self-centred and is in danger of destroying concepts such as loving relationships or compassion, for example. The concept of the good Samaritan has really disappeared. The good Samaritan acted out of pure altruism, love and all those things. The bloke in the ditch had no right to be picked up, but he was picked up out of charity. That's a concept which is going, I think.'

To illustrate this point, Warnock considers the question of disability rights.

'I think that the rather aggressive disablement lobby, for example, suggests that one is not allowed to pity or try to make things better for somebody with a disability, but that they as of right must be treated as absolute equals with everybody else. So it becomes very difficult to reintroduce the idea of helping somebody who is in difficulty or trying to make life better for somebody who is suffering from a disability, because the disabled lobby jumps up and says that's a patronising view and you've got to treat this person as exactly equal to yourself. I find it extremely difficult to handle, because it's an attitude of denial that there is such a thing as disability.'

Rights are not only claimed by the consumers of healthcare, but also by the providers. Thus, for example, it is often thought that doctors who are opposed to abortion have the right to refuse to carry them out, normally passing their patients on to other doctors. How far does the right to refuse treatment extend? Could a doctor refuse treatment for lung cancer to a smoker if they felt that the disease had been largely self-inflicted?

'My own feeling is that it would be a very dangerous path to travel down if treatments were in some way dependent upon the moral judgements doctors make about the character and behaviour of their patient,' Warnock replies. 'I suppose the only exception would be if we're talking about something like an assault on a doctor: I don't see why a doctor should treat somebody who has been violent towards him. But I do think if we begin to say, "Well, he brought it on himself," or "He was driving recklessly, so let's leave him to die" that would be terrible. For example, what happens if somebody has contracted syphilis through sexual adventures of various kinds? It seems to me that he must be treated. The doctor can't just say, "You shouldn't have done it so it's your fault."'

Making Babies is about much more than the question of rights, however. In it Warnock discusses several ethical issues concerning reproductive technologies and makes some controversial claims. One of these concerns sperm or egg donor anonymity. In 1984, her committee agreed that donor anonymity had to be preserved, mainly because if it were not, the number of people willing to come forward as donors would decrease. This evidence has so far not been replicated in the UK, when there is (in 2006) a severe shortage of donors. Subsequent experience in Scandanavia, however, suggests this is not in fact what happens when anonymity is removed. Warnock now not only argues for an end to anonymity, she describes the keeping secret of a child's biological origins as an 'evil'. Warnock explains that she was always uneasy about the committee's conclusion.

'The reason why I was uneasy has now become more important to me, which is that it's perfectly possible for parents to try and deceive altogether their child who was born by donation, largely because on the birth certificate the name of the non-biological father is given as the name of the father. I think there's a very strong case for having on the birth certificate "by donation" whether or not the name of the donor is to be given. I think it is an evil to bring a child up under a false impression or train him up in a false belief when the parents know the truth and the child is deceived. I didn't understand at the time how frequently this deception is attempted in the case of donation and I think that is something that ought to be legally brought to an end. It's no good just urging people to tell the child; you've got to take some definite step to make it impossible to deceive the child. Changing the rule about the birth certificate and opening up the same possibilities to children born of donation as are available to adopted children would solve this problem, I think.'

The use of the term 'evil' is extremely strong, especially for Warnock, who is known for the balance and moderation of her judgements. Why had she chosen such a strong word?

'Because it is deception of a very long-term kind,' she explains. 'There are two things. One is the strictly utilitarian objection to deception of this kind which is that the child is almost sure to suspect, find out, or have to be told and this will be a great shock and the cause of a loss of trust between parent and child. But secondly, on a more abstract level of morality, whether the child finds out or not it seems to me intrinsically wrong that anyone should be deceived in this radical way because it suggests that the child is being sacrificed, or at any rate his interests are being taken less seriously than the interests of the parents. And what is the point of the deception? Only that the child may not know that his social, or non-biological father was incapable of producing sperm or was in some way impotent.'

It is striking that in the original deliberations of the committee the consequentialist reasons for preserving donor anonymity – that it would lead to a decline in donors – seemed to have trumped in principle concerns about the possibility that children would be deceived by their parents. According to Warnock, this was partly because of a perception that there are proper limits on the extent to which government should interfere in child-rearing practices.

'It's actually very difficult to find any profound moral thinking of a personal kind in the committee's original report, because we were there just to advise ministers on public policy. Certainly we would all have thought it wrong to deceive a child, but this is not something that you can put into legislation. How people regard their children is not an issue of public policy. Or, at least, it wasn't then thought to be. Twenty years on, government is now much more intrusive, so there are rules about whether you can smack children or not, which there never would have been then. But it does seem to me that it is very difficult to argue in a public document like a committee report that there is an absolute moral prohibition on treating a child as less than rational, and therefore less than able to be trusted with facts about his heredity and his own father's ability or inability to produce sperm.

'The other thing is that in the last twenty years society in general has become far more accustomed to the idea that a child's genetic inheritance is of immense importance, both in forming who he is but also in his own perception of himself. I think we put far more emphasis now on the importance of the mix of genes that a person has than we did twenty years ago.'

Another controversial issue concerns the right of homosexuals to access reproductive technologies. Facilitating the growth of homosexual families is in Warnock's view a kind of social experiment, although not one that is ever going to be on a scale to radically alter the structure of society. She finds no reason to oppose this. This is perhaps surprising, since in her autobiography she describes herself as a natural conservative. But in this case she seems to be following Mill's liberal view that we should allow social experiments in living.

'It does sound like a sudden switch to believing in *On Liberty*, which I don't,' she concedes. 'I don't greatly admire that work, although I admire it in one way in that it was very bold and ground-breaking. I'm not sure that the contrast between conservative and liberal is terribly useful. I'm conservative in the sense that I don't believe that one can understand what's going on now or what ought to go on next unless one's got a very strong sense of history, how things arose and how they got to where they are. I'm greatly against, therefore, overthrowing without examining things that have taken root. But I think the argument here is that we really have very little evidence about what the effect on the child would be, and you really can't form moral judgements until you know what the facts are on the ground. Here we really don't. So one ought to allow this kind of experiment, which indeed it is, on the grounds that we know nothing against it.

'The only thing we do know from long experience is that a

child in care is almost certainly going to be a damaged child, whereas a child that is adopted into a loving homosexual family might well not be a damaged child. The same sort of argument would go to permit assisted birth for homosexuals: if children can flourish in that sort of situation then they should be allowed to. I know the parallel with adoption is not exact because the adopted child exists already. But if the parents want this child very much, and if it proves that they can manage children of this kind, then I have nothing against it, because I have nothing intrinsically against homosexuality.'

A third controversy concerns her argument that it may be acceptable to allow human cloning, albeit only in the case of total male infertility, and only if the technology becomes safe, which she thinks unlikely.

'My view is that it would be totally immoral to attempt human cloning as things are but if, almost inconceivably, the practical difficulties were overcome, then one would have to raise the question again: is there anything intrinsically awful about cloning? To which I replied, no, in certain circumstances. I think we may have to raise this question. In a way it's an evasion to say it's immoral because it's dangerous and people shouldn't experiment with other people; and also now it's illegal in this country so we have a kind of breathing space. I do think the question of whether it is intrinsically immoral will have to be faced very quickly, because I believe that the earliest cases of human cloning will come from the Far East. I think that in China they're forging ahead with this kind of experimentation, but it's very difficult to find out anything that's going on in China. I wouldn't be at all surprised if, within a decade, there were claims at any rate that human clones had been formed by cell nuclear replacement.

'One of the arguments against cloning is that every person

deserves, or has a right to, a mixture of genes from two parents. If cloning became fashionable, then doubtless there would be some damage to the gene pool, because it would not be constantly renewed by the chance mixing of genes that we get now. But really it is very unlikely that cloning will ever be widespread. For as long as humans exist, most people will go on having children in the ordinary way. But having said that there is an element of unpredictability here: one cannot foresee with absolute accuracy what damaged genes might arise out of an increase in the use of cloning.'

Talking to Warnock and reading her works, and in contrast with most works of moral philosophy, it is striking how much of what she says is based on what the facts are on the ground. One little-known fact she mentions in *Making Babies* is that artificially created clones are not one hundred per cent clones at all because of the small amount of DNA in the mitochondrial cells of the outer shell used to house the egg.

Does this emphasis on facts mark an important difference between the role of the professional ethicist and the moral philosopher?

'I still maintain that even in academic moral philosophy it is extremely valuable to understand what the facts are on the ground,' she replies. 'There has been an increasing use of real moral examples, all the way through the last century, at any rate from the 1950s onwards. I remember Jean Austin – J. L. Austin's widow – and I used to run a joint seminar in the early 1960s where we simply took moral difficulties and got people to say how they'd set about solving them and then examine what arguments they were overtly or unacknowledgedly solving them with. That was a fairly new thing to do then but I think it's become much more common, and it does entail thinking about all the facts. It's situational ethics, if you'd like to give it a name.'

This fits in with Warnock's wider view that the two hats she wears – the moral philosopher and the professional ethicist – conceal a deeper unity of purpose.

'I'd like to think that they were the same job in different contexts. I think there's a frightful danger in constantly bashing on in public about what ought or ought not to be the basis of legislation or whatnot, the kind of thing I do. There's a great danger that you tend to think that you never need go more deeply into the things that you're talking about. The combination of what would count as proper moral philosophy and what counts as this journalistic stuff is terribly difficult. I was very much interested in Onora O'Neill's two recent publications. One was the Reith Lectures and one was a book that came out just before, I think. She had addressed this very problem – how to combine accessibility with a decent degree of rigour and the answer to proper objections. It is a very hard act to combine these two things in proper proportion and I think that she manages it very well. But I'm not sure that I, out of laziness and old age, don't slither down into the journalism more often than I ought.'

Suggested Reading

Making Babies: Is There a Right to Have Children? (Oxford University Press)
A Memoir: People and Places (Duckworth)

10 Goodness

Philippa Foot

What is it that makes Philippa Foot one the best and most important moral philosophers of our age? Is it because she possesses a razor-sharp mind and the kind of analytic skill that enables her to dissect an argument at twenty paces? Not according to Foot. 'I have a certain insight into philosophy, but I'm not clever at all,' she says. 'I often don't find arguments easy to follow.' Is it her great scholarship? 'I don't read a lot, and I can't remember all these books and all their details; I'm undereducated really,' she confides. Is it because of the sheer volume of her output? Not when the hardback editions of her three published books would take up only two inches of your shelf space. Is it because she reflects the broader zeitgeist of contemporary ethical theory? Not when she has stood so resolutely opposed to the popular tides of 'expressivism' and the dogma of the is/ought gap, of which more later.

What makes Foot stand head and shoulders above almost all her peers is that her writing is thoughtful, insightful and is never about anything which is not important or interesting. Her work bears the hallmark of many of philosophy's best in that the reader can always gain something valuable by reading it, even if she profoundly disagrees with its conclusions.

Remarkably, Foot was already an octogenarian when her first ever monograph, *Natural Goodness*, was published in 2001.

This book represents the culmination of a lifetime of thought in ethics, which has been brought together in two collections: *Virtues and Vices* (containing essays from 1958 to 1977) and *Moral Dilemmas* (1977–2001). The intellectual route to *Natural Goodness* can be traced through these two collections, but the book represents the first ever bringing together of the various threads of her work into a mature, single vision of morality.

One way of getting a first grip on Foot's ideas is to start with her claim that morality begins with a recognition of the objective needs human beings have, needs which are of the same kind as those of plants and non-human animals. This is what 'natural goodness' means: 'What any living thing needs for its particular life,' as she puts it. 'Not individual needs – these could be anything such as a way out of prison – but what a living thing of that species needs given the habitat it lives in, which is much more determined for plants and other animals than it is for human beings.'

Foot thus bases her ethics on a recognition that facts about the world provide reasons for action. 'That children are born helpless and have to be taught to learn language and so on,' she explains, 'means already that children have to be looked after.'

Crucially, these reasons are 'objective and have nothing to do with preferences: some people love children and some people hate them. That doesn't make any difference.'

To those unfamiliar with recent moral philosophy this might seem unobjectionable, obvious even. But in fact it represents a direct challenge to two dogmas of ethical theory: the so-called 'is/ought gap' and what Foot calls the 'speaker-relative' account of moral judgement. Take the is/ought gap first. Those who maintain the existence of this gap – which is probably the majority of philosophers since Hume first described it in the eighteenth century – say that we can never derive any moral conclusions from merely descriptive facts. So, for example, from the fact that someone is suffering it can never follow logically that they ought to be helped. In order to get from the fact to the moral judgement you need to add something else, a general moral principle – for example, that suffering ought to be relieved. But this principle too cannot be derived from the facts alone.

How then does Foot bridge this gap? 'I've just done it in this discussion,' she says. 'From the fact that human children are not born able to do things, from this fact that they are born helpless, I get an ought: that they are to be looked after. Human beings need to look after children. That's an example of an is that gives an ought.'

This move can appear baffling, because it just seems to be a denial of the is/ought gap rather than a genuine counter-example. That is to say, someone who believes in the is/ought gap will just reply that the ought doesn't logically follow. A person who says that they know children are born helpless and need help but they don't see why they ought to give it may be morally culpable, but their logic is not at fault.

Foot, however, is not one to say something patently ridiculous, and to understand why her reply satisfies her and many of her admirers we need to consider her account of practical rationality: how we reason with regard to action. Here, Foot borrows a novel move suggested by her late friend and colleague Warren Quinn, to whom *Natural Goodness* is dedicated. Quinn's thought is that you need a conception of goodness in order to undertake practical rational deliberation at all: it is 'a necessary condition of practical rationality'.

'Practical rationality is taking the right things as reasons,' says Foot, 'so "the child is hungry" is a reason to feed it, and "smoking will kill you" is a reason for not taking up smoking.'

This can be compared to the alternative, orthodox view, which rests on an assumption that prudential self-interest is unproblematic as a reason for action, but to do anything other than for self-interested reasons presents a problem for practical rationality. Foot, in contrast, argues that practical rationality of all descriptions has to start by taking something as a reason for action and there is no logical reason why prudential self-interest is more of a reason to act than the needs of a child.

Her view can be summed up in the idea that moral reasoning is about practical rationality that recognizes the existence of objective human needs as reasons for action. What Foot thinks most significant about this is that it stands opposed to what she calls speaker-relative accounts of ethics found in theories such as emotivism, prescriptivism and subjectivism. She explains the contrast between her view and the speaker-relative one in some detail.

'Emotivism, expressivism and so on (all of them I lump together) think that there is something special in a moral judgement in the way that there is something special about an order. It's a special bit of language, like an avowal or a wish, or a greeting, although it isn't any of those things. These philosophers all ask, "What must the circumstances be for a moral word to be used by a speaker? What must he *desire*, what must he *want* others to do, what must he *feel*?" all of which are questions about the speaker. That is the right kind of question to ask about an order or a greeting, but I don't think that this sort of account is right for morality at all. I say that what we've got to dig out in order to understand a moral judgement is a particular use of the word "good", and that is nothing to do with what the speaker wants. It's not dependent on conditions in the speaker, so mine is not a speaker-relative account.

'So I'm really talking about a general concept of "good" that applies to plants, animals and human beings. You can't understand what I mean when I say I think it is acting badly to break a promise until you first understand that "good" is used of living things in a particular way. It's not like "oh good" which is speaker-relative and it's not like "good vacuum cleaner" either, which really depends upon the interests of people who use these things. But it belongs only to living things.

'So first I identify this very general sense of good, then I try to explain it by its relation to the particular things which beings of that kind, living species, need to do just to survive. You're defective if you don't do that. A hedgehog that ran from a predator would be defective, a deer that made itself as small as possible would be defective. That doesn't mean that just by chance it might not be the one that survives but nevertheless that's not the way in which a deer defends itself.

'I'm moving in upon this quite alternative account which has no truck with conditions in the speaker. And when we're thinking about plants and animals we're not worried about objectivity at all. It's an objective fact that a fleeing hedgehog would be a defective hedgehog.'

To show that a person's own present desires and wishes are not needed to generate an 'ought', Foot introduces the example of a teenager who we say ought not to start smoking.

'The teenager might query our ought, but wouldn't they be wrong? We take it as a reason and that's what the ought is saying: that they do have a reason to stop. They might say, "I don't care now" and they are rejecting your ought, but they're wrong because they do have a reason to stop. This case makes it easier to see that there is something strange about thinking that an ought depends on feeling, desire or whatever. Right now they don't have any such feelings and doesn't that destroy the idea that an ought, a value, needs a desire?'

A possible objection here is that the existence of a reason for doing something – for example, stopping smoking – does not seem to be sufficient to generate the conclusion that one *ought* to do that thing. What then would make it a *sufficient* reason?

'It's that the reason is the kind of reason that if you don't do it then you'll be acting badly,' Foot replies. 'This is about the difference between the moral judgement that really is a must, and you'll be acting badly if you don't act in accordance with it, and the moral judgement that says it would be good to do a certain thing, that there is a good reason for doing it, but we haven't got this compulsion.

'There is some circularity here, and that's because there is a connection of meaning between 'should' used in this sense and the idea that you act badly if you don't act in this way. So if I say something like you should give up smoking, then I'm saying that you are acting badly, imprudently, if you don't give up. So there are these connections of meaning. However, I'm not *basing* one on the other; I'm just saying that there is this connection.

'It is genuinely complicated because there are a lot of things, such as giving all your money to Oxfam, that you are not bad if you don't do them. But there are other cases where if you say you should do something, then you're saying you're bad if you do not. However, we mustn't lose sight of the important point here, which has to do with the demystification of "should" and "ought" by taking them to mean to do what is good for one's health, family, future, children, and country perhaps. At no point does it seem that you have to talk about speakers' attitudes.'

If then, for example, you confront a smoker in their forties, and they just say they don't want to give up, they're aware of the risks, but they are prepared to accept them and carry on smoking – are they making a mistake?

'It depends on what they say,' Foot replies. 'If they follow Hume and say that it is not contrary to reason to prefer one's own lesser good to one's greater good, then they are making a mistake: it *is* contrary to reason. But it's a different matter if the person says "I'll jolly well go on doing it and you're not going to stop me. You haven't told me anything that is going to affect me." So it would depend on what is said as to whether a mistake is being made or not.'

The example of stopping smoking might strike some people as being redundant, since the decision to smoke or not to smoke does not seem to be a moral but a prudential one. 'Prudence, as wisdom, is a virtue, you know,' Foot retorts. 'It's a very modern thing to try to distinguish the moral.' Critics risk missing the point of Foot's approach if they bring with them the presumption that, if we talk about reasons for action, there are going to be fixed points at which we suddenly move from the factual to the prudential and then into the moral. On Foot's view, this doesn't happen.

'Absolutely,' she agrees when this is put to her. 'Human beings are defective if their sight is so bad that they can't see other human beings or recognize faces, for instance. But they're also defective if they don't look after their children. But people tend to think, "Ah, but now we've gone to the moral, because it's not just about keeping oneself alive, it's keeping one's children alive."'

Foot argues that her view provides an objective morality. This rings alarm bells for many contemporary ethical theorists who think the idea of an objective morality is an outmoded dream. The objectivity is provided by the fact that human needs are real, regardless of our desires or preferences. So what about the objection that what is needed for a human life doesn't seem to be something you could hope to get an objective answer to in the way that you can for a plant, for example, simply because humans have a range of different desires, motivations, interests and so on?

'We live in different cultures. The habitat is much more varied than it is for other living things, and the range of conditions in which human beings can live given their ability to make clothes, and houses, heat and so on, is obviously much greater,' she replies. 'And given we are emotional beings, we have a whole lot of very subtle interests: the family is not just for reproduction, people want different things and there are different cultures. But that is not in favour of subjectivity at all. It only means that you've got to differentiate. Certain things are absolutely certain – that the young are helpless and so are the old – they don't just die suddenly, they get ill and infirm and need help. These are facts for all human beings. They don't do well being very lonely. When Freud said that love and work are the only two real therapies, I think that he said something quite generally true about human beings.

'So neither the fact that there is a differentiation in the detail of what is needed in a particular society, culture, or even climates, nor the fact that things are not going to be cut and dried, makes for subjectivity. If it moves towards relativism it's just a kind of cultural relativism. It isn't basic relativism as beloved by first-year students.'

Foot is confident that differentiation is sufficient to accommodate the variety of human preferences and that only 'irreconcilability in principle' would threaten her objective framework. Difficult cases pose no such threat. 'It doesn't matter in the least that there is not an answer to every question.' But she cannot see any compelling examples of such irreconcilability. 'The idea that because people have different preferences you can move to the conclusion that there must be a radical breakdown of discussion about good and bad action – that's exactly what I deny and can't let past. Some people care about art and some people don't. Some people want public money spent one way and some people don't. You don't conclude "so subjectivism".'

Some of Philippa Foot's closest philosophical friends have been Roman Catholics. The late Elizabeth Anscombe, her colleague and inspiration, was one, as are the Dummetts. Foot herself, however, is a 'card-carrying atheist'. I asked her about the role of fundamental, non-philosophical convictions in the formation of philosophical beliefs.

'Both Elizabeth Anscombe and Michael Dummett are much, much better philosophers than me,' she says. 'You can be a jolly good philosopher and still not be in their league. I once asked Michael, "What happens when your argument goes one way and your religious belief goes the other?" And he said, "How would it be if you knew that something was true? Other things would have to fit with it." That, I take it, is the clue, that they think they *know* that and could as little deny it as that I am talking to someone now.'

In her own case, she carries with her a fundamental conviction of another kind. 'I'll tell you a bit of biography. During the war I went to London to work as an economist, and then I came back and started to work on philosophy. I was just really getting going on moral philosophy when the photographs and films of Belsen and Birkenau came out, and it's really not possible to convey to people who are younger what it was like. One would have said such a thing on that scale could not happen, human beings couldn't do this. That was what was behind my refusing to accept subjectivism even when I couldn't see any way out. It took a long time and it was only in the last fifteen or twenty years that I managed it. But I was certain that it could not be right that the Nazis were convinced and that there was no way that they were wrong. It just could not be.

'That's why I could never accept Charles Stevenson, say,

whose emotivism implies that in the end you simply express one attitude and I express another. Sure, there's all that finding out about the facts and so on, but in the end it is just that. I was not going to swallow this, in spite of really only being able to chip away at it. So there is something that has driven all my moral philosophy: the Holocaust, and the shock that it was to someone in their twenties that it could have happened.'

What then would Foot say to the person who claims to be an emotivist, and yet says that they are vehemently opposed to the Holocaust; that they consider it a barbarism? Is there something not true in what they're saying?

'No, they've just got their philosophy wrong,' she replies. 'Somehow we must be able to show that the Nazis were just wrong, that they were making mistakes, saying things that weren't true. I don't think the emotivists have done much harm, whereas certainly I've been accused of doing a lot of harm because I encouraged people to think there was objectivity and then when they discovered there wasn't, they would throw morality out of the window.'

It would be hard for a young philosopher starting out today to have a career like Foot's, since there is now so much pressure on them to publish as much as possible. 'I didn't ever have to publish,' admits Foot. 'In fact in those days I think people asked those who published a lot why they did so. One had a job for life and a college stood behind one.'

Foot's work could only have come out of this kind of environment where thoughts are given time to gel and develop. A lot of papers published in philosophy today are good at the mental gymnastics, but they don't necessarily get at the nub of the issue. There's a certain perceptiveness in Foot about what is at stake and what is important. Is that mode of philosophizing under threat from the way that academic philosophy is going now, when people have to produce more and more quickly?

'Yes, I think so,' says Foot, 'with these awful official reviews there's much too much out. Philosophy is also going in a slightly technical direction, I think. I couldn't have done that. I have a certain insight into philosophy, I think. But I'm not clever, I don't find complicated arguments easy to follow.'

Foot also shows a healthy disregard for the need to show a wide command of the current 'literature' on any given subject. 'I can't remember all these books and all their details. I think I've done philosophy through discussion and reading just a few great things over and over again. I couldn't tell you about some philosophers, such as Spinoza. I'm very uneducated really. But one learns from one's pupils, graduate students, and I learned from marvellous colleagues at UCLA.'

Foot talks fondly of her long conversations with colleagues such as Elizabeth Anscombe ('she must have been putting to me the questions that Wittgenstein put to her. Practically every day we talked for hours. I was incredibly lucky'). If she feels fortunate then so must her interlocutors, since she is a generous and insightful discussant.

'It's a very peculiar and rather painful way of doing philosophy,' she says, 'because I really am terribly ignorant about much philosophy, I have a terrible memory and I don't do it in quite the way clever people who have very good memories and are splendid scholars do it.'

For which we should say, thank goodness for that, since Foot's particular approach has yielded one of the most distinctive and valuable contributions to contemporary moral philosophy.

Suggested Reading

Virtues and Vices (Oxford University Press)
Natural Goodness (Oxford University Press)
Moral Dilemmas (Oxford University Press)

11 Love

The Soho Symposium

I was just coming out of Foyles bookshop on London's Charing Cross Road when I ran into the editor of *The Philosophers' Magazine*. It transpired that like me he was on his way to the launch of Michael Bywater's book, *Lost Worlds*, being held at the remnant of one such world, Wilton's Music Hall in the East End. That much I later discovered, for at the time I confessed I knew little about the book or the venue for the party.

'Basically, the book is about all the things, great and small, that no longer exist,' the editor informed me, 'such as the dodo, the father's favourite armchair and woollen swimming costumes. I'm not sure if he mentions them, but I would also have thought symposiums belong to the category of lost worlds. Of course, businesspeople and academics organize what they call symposiums. But they are nothing like the gatherings of Ancient Greece, with food, wine, flute-girls, libations and so forth.'

'Has the symposium really vanished?' I replied. 'Didn't you yourself organize one? Joseph Chandler told me once about a kind of symposium that you and Michael were involved in a while back. Apparently, you were trying to decide whether a young woman would be advised to fall in love or steer well clear of it. He also said that a fairly vicious fight broke out between two of the philosophers present about the scope of Darwinian explanations.'

The editor laughed. 'That's not quite how I remember it,' he said, 'though I have learned not to trust even my own memories entirely. But there is some truth in what Joseph told you. Of course, there were no flute-girls or libations. But there was food, drink and a lively, sometimes heated discourse on the nature of love.'

I asked if he would give me his account of how he remembered it. Since there was a good hour to spare before the launch party and it was being held on the other side of town, he agreed to tell me what he remembered as we walked across the city. I believe him to be a trustworthy witness, though his caution about the weakness of memory needs to be doubly restated, as his account has also suffered from the distortions of my own recollection of our conversation. This, in any case, is what I remember of what he told me.

*   *   *   *   *

We had gathered in a restaurant in Soho, an area notorious for its devotion to Eros, if not the other gods of love. Most of the guests were not well-known to each other. I had invited them all because I thought they would have very different perspectives on the subject of love, which was the topic I had chosen for us to discuss. I remember it took a little time for everyone to really relax and offer their thoughts uninhibited. Fortunately, one of the guests was the philosopher Peter Cave, who is never backwards about coming forwards. So it was that he kicked off our discussion with his reflections on love. This is more or less what he said:

'There is an exchange in Samuel Beckett's play, *Endgame*, in which Clov asks Hamm, "Do you believe in a life to come?" Hamm replies, "All mine's been a life to come."

'The exchange reminds me of love, or at least of erotic love, or at least of what lovers strive after. Love involves both a quest for an end, one of permanence; yet, it seems, an inevitable endlessness to that quest – or even a giving up on the quest.

'I'm also reminded of love by Kafka's tale of the poor man who seeks access to the law. What gives him hope is the existence of a gate to the law, despite the presence of an oppressive doorkeeper barring his way. The doorman accepts a bribe from the applicant – but only so the applicant knows he had not left anything undone. Eventually the doorkeeper slams the gate shut in the man's face.

'Many of us seek love, as the poor man seeks justice, as a life to come; indeed, we tend to pity those who lack love and pity those who lack the desire for love. Sometimes we find love – we breathe in the ecstasy, it colours our world – yet we often know that we live an erotic fiction: our very biology slams the gate shut on any permanence.

'Love involves an incongruity between two perspectives: the Parmenidean – "All is one; there is no motion" – and the Heraclitean – "Everything is in flux." Love, on the one hand, has the aim of safety, stability, unity, eternity, the past – "We were meant for each other"; "Whatever happens, I shall always love you" – yet, on the other hand, love promotes changes, uncertainties, jealousies, a drawing together of incompatibles (typically the incompatibility of man and woman). We seek love's mountain tops, blue skies, an eternal togetherness that soars beyond the daily contingencies; yet, fleshy, developing, see-sawing biological monads that we are, we can attain no such transcendence.

'Erotic love, more mundanely, engages us in bodily intimacies, explorations and revelations; in flying kites, stretching the eyes, rhapsodising the moon. Yet it also involves losses and fears. It's the hope that gets us: our search for the bliss of the union generates our vulnerability to another. This might lead me to recommend the life of a pebble; but, of course, that would be no life at all. Breathing love's paradoxes at least keeps one amused.

'Plato argued that the tragic dramatist should also be a comic poet. An appreciation of love's quest requires us to see both how it ensnares us in the tragic, yet also in absurdity. As Dennis the Menace from the *Beano* says, after watching a film, 'He didn't really kiss her … they've got stuntmen for that kind of stuff.'

'Reflect on how seriously we treat the funny business we do with each other's body, yet how comical it is. As Schopenhauer said, 'Love knows how to slip its love-notes and ringlets into ministerial portfolios and philosophical manuscripts. Every day it brews and hatches the worst and most perplexing quarrels and dispute.' There is the urgency in sexual desire, yet *le petit morte* follows.'

Peter's speech stirred many thoughts and questions in the minds of those present, but it was agreed that we should hear what everyone had to say in turn without interruption before launching into a discussion. So it was that Ellie Levenson, a young journalist whose columns often touch on themes of love, shared her thoughts with the assembled company.

'I should start with a confession. I am not sure that I have ever been in love. Nevertheless this won't stop me talking about it. It seems to me that love really is some kind of mental illness, uncontrollable and frightening, though perhaps with some good elements too. With love, rationality and logic take a back seat.

'I don't know that any musings on love can ever be complete without some kind of poetry, and I immediately thought of D. H. Lawrence's poem, "A Young Wife", which begins "The pain of loving you is almost more than I can bear".

'Although Lawrence wouldn't approve of my interpretation, to me, "the pain of loving you" isn't referring to the fine line between love and hate, or pain and joy, but the feeling, and the anguish, of being an essentially rational being caught up in a mental state where rationality is irrelevant.

'When I was a teenager I had an infatuation with a friend. We developed an extremely close friendship which hung on our enjoyment of talking rubbish about books, drinking red wine and smoking a bit of cannabis. Over time my crush developed and I became convinced that I loved this person. I laugh at myself now, but I used to think, in that way that teenagers do, that if a gunman were to walk into a room we were both in and say one of us must die, I would choose myself because his life was worth more than mine.

'I thought this was love. I understand now that it was just teenage melancholy. But maybe it was love, because love is different for all people. Because love is an emotion, not an object, it is impossible to know if one person's love is the same as another's. So what for one person is love, may to me be lust, or to another infatuation. So it strikes me that love has to be self-defining. We can't tell someone if they are in love, we cannot agree or disagree when someone tells us they love us or another. If someone thinks they are in love, then they are in love.

'In the musical, *Fiddler on the Roof*, Tevye the milkman asks his wife, Golde, "Do you love me?" She seems puzzled by the question: "I'm your wife," she replies.

'"I know … But do you love me?" Tevye insists. And Golde sings:

"Do I love him? For 25 years I've lived with him, fought him, starved with him. Twenty-five years my bed is his, if that's not love, what is?"

'I was talking about tolerance with someone the other day, commenting on living in a shared house, and saying that I am getting to the point in my life where I only want my books on the bookshelves. My companion asked what would I do when I have a partner. And we came to the conclusion that perhaps that is a good definition of love for the pseudo-intellectual such as myself – someone who you don't mind sharing your bookshelf with. If that's not love, what is?'

The claim that only the lover can judge if they were in love raised the hackles of some of the philosophers, who wanted to insist that people can think they are in love and be mistaken. And Ellie herself confessed to a possible counter-example to her final thought: it had taken ten years of marriage before one couple she knew agreed that they didn't need to buy two copies of books they both wanted to read. Perhaps aided by the second bottle of Chateau Haut Guillon Bordeaux, opinions were being offered more readily than before. But the resolution to hear everyone in turn more or less uninterrupted was restated. And so it was the turn of another philosopher, Helena Cronin, who now had competition for the attention of those present in the form of the gorgonzola stuffed mushrooms and vegetable soup which arrived just as she began her speech.

'I'm going to tell you what the very best of modern science knows about love. The question is "What is love?" And the answer is, of course, Darwinian. Love is an adaptation, evolved by natural selection. You then have to ask what the adaptation is for; and then how it works, what its mechanisms are.

'The answer to the question of what love is for is very simple and rather mundane: it's all for the sake of the children. Love is designed to keep future fathers and mothers together. The offspring in our species come into the world utterly unable to fend for themselves; they require a huge burden of care, unceasing vigilance, a never-ending stream of resources. And they stay that way for a long, long time. Ancestrally, mothers couldn't manage this alone. So it paid fathers to invest in them, to provide resources and protection. That is why natural selection has favoured both sexes with our treasured ability to form deep and long-lasting attachments – to fall in love.

'Love is therefore a human universal. So, contrary to a widely held myth, romantic love is not a modern, European invention. It is part of our evolved human nature. So, for example, in all societies worldwide we find evidence of it in the culture. There's always a specific word for love in the local language, always love songs, and always folk tales about romantic entanglements.

'Now to the question: how does this adaptation work? It comes in two stages: romantic love and companionate love. Romantic love is what both Peter and Ellie apparently had in mind; and both of them were rather cynical about the fact that it doesn't persist. But it's not designed to persist. Romantic love brings potential parents together; it is companionate love that keeps people together. And the two adaptations work in very different ways. The thing about romantic love is that it signals credible commitment. You are committed to your loved one not because you've made a rational calculation that she's got the right waist-to-hip ratio, or he's got the right bank balance. You may well take those things into account. But, if that were all there was, the object of your love would be vulnerable; for you might soon find someone else who scores even better on your check-list. Romantic love solves this problem because, above and beyond the check-list, you fall in love with someone because it is them. One of the most intriguing pieces of evidence for this is that even someone who is in love with an identical twin doesn't fall in love with the other twin.'

Helena had some more to say about companionate love, but what I have just told you provided the real heart of her message. Having fulfilled her oratory obligations, she was free at last to set upon the fungi that had been slowly cooling in front of her.

Her Darwinian intervention had certainly sown the seeds for some discontent which was to emerge later. But once again, we resisted entering into a fierce debate prematurely as two more guests remained to speak. The order of their doing so was settled by the most pragmatic criterion: whereas Anthony Price was still eating his starter, Michael Bywater had polished his off. So it was that the writer and journalist said something like this:

'I'm not sure that talking about design doesn't lead us down all sorts of blind alleys. But so does everything else. Everything we think and talk, believe, experience, feel, see, hear and are told about love turns out to be wrong.

'One of the problems with love is whether we're talking about *eros*, *agape*, *philia* or *storge*. If we move to the Latin chop it's neater: between *amor* – the erotic, sexual love between adults – and *caritas*, the caring love between friends and families. A couple of years ago I saw an advertisement on the Paris metro for Dim tights. It showed a woman with endless legs, a very short skirt, very high red heels, probably Manolo Blahnik by the look of them, wearing these tights. This image of absolute erotic power would never be seen in our society, because there was another person in the picture, clutching her around the thigh. This person was a toddler, obviously her child. *Amor* and *caritas* were combined in a way which we find hard to imagine.

'That reflects the fact that love is a fractal phenomenon. Fractals are things which show the same pattern of order or randomness at whatever scale you look at them. Think of a coastline drawn big on a map. It goes in, it goes out, it's jagged, it curves. Look at a bit of coastline closer up. It does the same thing at a smaller scale. Look at it even closer still. It does the same thing. Look at a leaf, look at most biological systems and they're fractals. Love behaves like a fractal. However closely we look, it seems to show the same pattern of desires, illogicalities and compulsions. It's too broad for us to understand and it's too fractal for us to understand.

'Suppose we do try to understand it. Imagine I am God, working through natural selection, creating a species with a high-investment reproductive strategy. The first thing I have to do is get sex right: I have to make sure that male A and female B meet, form a bond, breed and look after their children long enough for life to go on. To lapse into the Anglo-Saxon, I need to get these two exemplars of the species to fuck and then stick together. But the first thing to do is to get them into bed. Once that's achieved I can allow them to evolve lovely things like art, culture, poetry, music, philosophy, love, fidelity, constancy and so on. But first I must get them into the sack, drive them temporarily mad, get them to make a ridiculous commitment to each other, to believe against all possibility of denial that each to the other is special, the two sundered halves that have found themselves over the whole wide world.

'To again use the Anglo-Saxon, we have to remember that the bit of us that fucks isn't the bit of us that thinks. So when we try to think about love, which stems from sexual reproduction, we find it hard to think about it because at the core of this is a desire which has nothing to do with the bit of us that thinks. The core problem of love is that we think it is the generation of a consistent mind, and we do not have a consistent mind.'

I am afraid that I have left out a great deal of what Michael said, perhaps even the most interesting parts. What we remember is so often only that which in some way connects with other memories, so that the web of recollection helps to sustain itself. So it is that of the many mental fireworks Michael lit, only those that flashed direct illumination on the contributions of the other speakers burned themselves into my memory. Still, I am in some ways surprised to have remembered as much as I have. I have often wondered if my memory is worse than it used to be. If it were so, however, I would hardly be able to remember how good it used to be.

So we finally came to our last speaker, a third philosopher, Anthony Price. His starter devoured, we gave him the opportunity to get his piece in before the main course arrived. What he really wanted to do was disagree with Michael and Helena. However, he resolved instead to deliver the speech he had originally intended to give.

'For the analyst, adolescent love is a re-enactment of the mental processes by which the child made his world a home. Because he loved his mother, he perceived her as loving him, which is simple projection. Also because he loved her, he perceived her as lovable, which is complex projection. Because he was afraid to lose her, he incorporated her in phantasy within himself, thus forming his first, and most positive, ego-ideal. Of course, this is the rosy side of things. To the extent that he also hated her, and blamed her for being insecurely his own, he projected, and introjected, bad qualities and objects.

'But that is lost, and recoverable only speculatively. The adolescent re-enacts it in a new context of which he will always retain a memory, and in new forms that lend themselves to articulation. He thus recovers a conscience, and gains an intelligent awareness of the nature that he shares with the child that he was. Falling in love is always a self-revelation.

'Can it also be a revelation of the other? It is a familiar thought that it can't be, and the theme is recurrent in Proust, who takes the lover to know less than anyone about the beloved. However, our desires enjoy a remarkable plasticity, and – like the Lesbian rule cited by Aristotle – can adapt themselves to objects rather than adapting objects, in the manner of Procrustes, to themselves. Here Molière, in *Le Misanthrope*, is a corrective: "Their passion never sees aught to blame in it, and in the beloved all things become loveable. They think their faults perfections, and invent sweet terms to call them by." Such a love re-evaluates what is there to be perceived. A purely idealizing love, which re-creates the beloved anew, expresses either ignorance, or hatred, of what she is actually like.

'Both these responses, of idealization or of re-evaluation, fall under Stendhal's concept of *cristillization*, "that action of the mind that discovers fresh perfections in its beloved at every turn of events". In this manner, every new discovery about the beloved, and every new situation in which she can be imagined, becomes a new reason for loving her. As Stendhal cites, "One of your friends breaks his arm hunting; how sweet it is to receive the care of a woman whom one loves!"

'While the idealizing aspect of love is the replica of an infantile attachment, its re-evaluative aspect becomes the prototype of a Christian love which takes as its object not one person as one would wish her to be, but all humans as they actually are, in all their concreteness. Erotic love thus becomes the bridge between the irrecoverable starting-point, and the unimaginable end-point, of human love at its most imperative.'

*   *   *   *   *

By the time the editor had finished telling me about all the speeches we were already close to the Tower of London and so were near to our destination.

'But what of the fracas about Darwinism and the question about whether it is advisable to fall in love?' I asked. 'Are these complete fictions?'

'Not at all,' replied the editor. 'There was much more discussed after the speeches were given, and if we had longer I could tell you a great deal about them, even though I have forgotten more still. The problem with describing the fracas, as you describe it, is that it was not so much an incident as a kind of intellectual storm that raged in the background of the whole gathering. It's hard to put one's finger on what was really at its core. My own view is that the issue was about fitness for purpose. No one was denying that human beings are how they are at least partly because of how we have evolved. But the majority wanted to protest that any historical and biological account of how we came to be how we are is going to leave a great deal of what we now want to know about love unilluminated. For example, nothing about the evolutionary causes of our feelings of love can tell us if love is good or of value.

'So really the issue was about what kinds of explanation Darwinian accounts are fit to give and what they must leave for other approaches. But even this, I have to say, doesn't quite explain the ferocity of some of the debate. Those who saw the attempts at Darwinian explanations as extending over too wide a territory were outraged at what they saw as the incursion, while the invaders themselves, to use an unfair metaphor, found the resistance to their methods baffling. People say rather misleadingly that Darwin saw nature as red in tooth and claw. But it is undoubtedly true that today, debates about Darwin are almost invariably bloody. Isn't it extraordinary that Darwin still provokes such hostility and disagreement one-and-a-half centuries after the publication of his earth-shattering work?'

'Indeed it is,' I replied. 'But tell me, what was your own role in this? Weren't you too called to make a speech?' The editor laughed.

'My friend, why do you think I am the editor of a philosophy magazine rather than a philosopher? I am an intellectual parasite. I attach myself to philosophers, suck from them what I can and then regurgitate it in digestible form for others. I myself have nothing to contribute, only to redistribute.

'However, I did make one intervention at the end of the discussion, which concerns your second question. Having listened to what everyone had to say, I found myself wondering what use these reflections were to people in love. The question was echoed by another raised by Ellie, who you will recall confessed that she thought she had never been in love at all. What would people advise her? Should she fall in love?

The problem struck me as one concerning the possibility of romanticism. Romanticism, to my mind, is unfairly ridiculed by those who fancy themselves to be intellectual. That is because people mistake it for naïve idealism and unrealistic expectations. But to my mind, romanticism is not the view that everyone will live happily ever after. To be romantic is to maintain that, even though love is merely a biological adaptation, even though it defies rational control, even though it is not permanent, even though it must contain the bitter as well as the sweet; still, love is valuable and worth having. To be truly romantic is not to give up on love, even when the mist has been removed from our eyes and we see it for the paradoxical, illogical, biological mess that it is. In other words, we are romantic if we could leave our symposium, having said all we have said, still affirming the value of love.

'I asked all the participants if they could do that, and by extension, whether they would advise Ellie to hold out for love or flee from it as soon as it rears its head. Peter replied in the affirmative, remarking that we need to embrace the paradox and absurdity or else we end up with the life of the pebble. Helena agreed that Ellie should be open to love, saying that, even though there are negative aspects to it, nevertheless, by helping us to understand love, science can help to ameliorate these aspects and enable us to enjoy it as part of the rich cornucopia of human nature. Anthony also answered the question with a qualified yes, saying that we can transform the reality of human life by the attitudes we take to it, and that some forms of romantic love can enrich life to make it more worthwhile. Finally, although Michael agreed with that, he wanted to say that the question itself was muddle-headed as it implied we have a choice. The truth is that love comes when it comes, and we do not choose whether to succumb to it or not.'

With that we turned into Grace's Alley, a mere few yards from our destination. The silhouette of Michael could be seen down the lane, hobbling on a stick as a result of a collision with a scooter in Rome. Perhaps I would ask him for his version of events, though that would have to wait for another day.

I should mention, however, the destination itself. Wilton's Music Hall is a building to bring out the romantic in anyone. It belongs to a lost world, yet its survival is a sign that, in fact, all is not lost, just as the modern-day symposium the editor told me about showed that the customs of Ancient Greece were not completely lost either. Perhaps indulgently, I allowed these romantic thoughts to apply themselves to the subject of love. People build theatres, like they did the Parthenon, and they fall in love. All decay and eventually vanish altogether. But it takes a long time for all to be completely lost. Even when love is gone, something of it remains. It may not be eternal and unchanging, but it is persistent, insistent and will not allow reason to banish it.

With apologies to Plato and the memory of his classic Symposium.

The Symposiasts

Michael Bywater is a writer and broadcaster and the author of *Lost Worlds* and *Big Babies* (Granta).
Peter Cave is an associate lecturer in philosophy for the Open University, and some time ago co-author of numerous pieces of erotica.

Helena Cronin is co-director of the Centre for Philosophy of Natural and Social Science at the London School of Economics, where she runs Darwin@LSE, and is author of *The Ant and The Peacock* (Cambridge University Press).

Ellie Levenson is a former editor of the *Fabian Review* and a freelance journalist.

Anthony Price is a reader in philosopher at Birkbeck College, University of London, and author of *Love and Friendship in Plato and Aristotle* (Oxford University Press).

Bernard Williams

Just before I left Bernard Williams' Oxford home, with my tape recorder packed away and interview completed, the man many call Britain's greatest living philosopher told me a story about a colleague who gave a lecture in Germany. At the end of the talk, a student came up to him and told him how impressed he was and how he'd like to 'join his school'. However, it could not be. 'Unfortunately,' he explained, 'I am a Kantian.'

If you don't find the anecdote amusing then it's very possible you're not going to be impressed by Williams's philosophy, to which the 'systems' and 'positions' of so many Teutonic professors are anathema. The effect of reading a Bernard Williams book is not that you can now state what his positions are on topics X, Y and Z, but that you understand things better. Is that something he's happy about?

'Yes,' says Williams. 'In general I guess that's because I think that philosophy starts from realizing we don't understand our own activities and thoughts. What I think most about is showing people that we don't understand our own thoughts, and then suggesting and opening up ways in which we might get a better hold of them.

'One of the nicest things ever said about my philosophy came from someone who proceeds in a quite different way, and he said to me that he thought it was liberating, because it stopped people having to think within a certain box where something seems absolutely essentially connected to something else. I like that, if that's right.'

Some have found that quality irritating, including his former tutor, Richard Hare, who found Williams too negative. 'Dick would say, "You knock all this stuff down, what do you put in its place?"' recalls Williams. 'Of course my immediate answer is, in *that* place I don't put anything. That isn't a place anything should be.'

Most of his contemporaries would judge this to be a strength rather than a weakness of his work, and his stature among his peers is evidenced by the fact that his critics and admirers are often one and the same.

Now in his seventies, Williams is as sharp and productive as ever, and has just published a substantive monograph, *Truth and Truthfulness*. It's vintage Williams: elegantly written, full of insight, and devoid of any pat answers or artificially clear-cut conclusions.

'It's about what I call the virtues of truth,' explains Williams, 'and I mean by those, obviously, virtues of people which are associated with the truth. I identify two basic ones, which I label – and they are labels – accuracy and sincerity. The virtues of accuracy are those connected with finding out the truth, trying to get things right and so forth; and the virtues of sincerity are those of communicating them to other people in an honest way: saying what you believe and so on.'

The book is subtitled *An Essay in Genealogy*, a deliberate allusion to Nietzsche's *The Genealogy of Morals*. Like Nietzsche's classic, Williams' book combines real history and fictional constructs to tell a revealing story that makes us reconsider the meaning of familiar concepts.

'I have a construction in which these two basic virtues of truth are derived from certain absolutely essential features of human communication,' he explains. 'I put that in what I call, as in the tradition of political philosophy, a state of nature story, about a very simple society in which people have a fundamental division of labour about finding out various things.'

This fictional, abstract part of the story is supplemented by real history.

'The idea is that although you can make these absolutely schematic, basic needs for such virtues clear at the level of what I call the state of nature – that is, by pure reflection on the needs of human communication – they are, in fact, to an enormous degree changed, transformed, differently embodied, extended and so on by historical experience. And a fundamental claim of the book is a methodological one, namely that if we're going to understand the puzzles that surround these concepts now – and there are many such problems in our present time – you can only understand them through a historical knowledge of the concept.'

Williams is very keen to distinguish his historical method from certain other armchair attempts to understand our present by means of our past. 'I make it very clear that the state of nature is not supposed to be an *a priori* exercise in evolutionary psychology, a subject about which I have very considerable suspicions anyway.' So what is it that evolutionary psychology leaves out?

'The most essential and obvious fact about the human species, which has given it enormous power, is that it has acquired the power of non-genetic learning. That is, there are cultural transmissions from one generation to another that are cumulative. In the course of this, culture starts going its own way. To understand those cultures is to understand what being a human being has made possible. You can't understand them by going back to the most basic apparatus that enables anybody to have any culture at all. That is itself an element.'

One question that dogs both genealogical enquiries and evolutionary psychology is the extent to which understanding the origins of a custom or concept debunks it and leaves it hollow. In the case of morality, the concern is that the genealogy is 'disobliging': it takes away the 'ought' from moral judgements. In this respect, Williams and Nietzsche part company.

'Nietzsche's genealogy of morality is disobliging. That is, it's an unmasking operation. If you're convinced by it, you don't think as well of morality as you did when you started. Alasdair MacIntyre, in *Three Methods of Moral Inquiry*, actually identifies genealogy with a hostile, unmasking, deconstructive method, as on the whole did Foucault, although there are more qualifications required there. I don't accept that identification. I think that some genealogies are disobliging. Indeed I think Nietzsche was right and that the genealogy of what he specifically calls morality is disobliging.

'By contrast with this, take Hume's famous derivation of the "artificial virtues of justice", which is actually an example of genealogy in my sense. Hume introduces the notion of the state of nature and he says, "and this we may use so long as it be granted that it be a fiction". I don't think you have to accept Hume's view. The point is that if you accepted it you wouldn't have any reason to think worse of justice.'

Williams' genealogy does not in any sense diminish the idea of truth. Indeed, one of its main goals is to show us just how essential the idea of truth is. Here, Williams weighs in against the 'deniers', who in a variety of ways say 'all these things we value and are interested in have got nothing to do with the truth at all. There isn't any truth or there isn't any objective truth or if there is truth we can't get at it.'

However, and as one of the most influential deniers in philosophy, Richard Rorty, pointed out in his review of *Truth and Truthfulness* in the *London Review of Books*, Williams actually agrees with much of what the deniers say. It's just that he sees a gap between what is right in their arguments and the radically sceptical nature of their conclusions.

For example, Williams says, 'Sometimes the deniers mean the absolutely platitudinous truth that given the subject matter, even given an object, there is no one story to be told about it which is the truth about it. Well that's certainly correct. Just take a stone or a glass of water: there are umpteen stories to be told about it. But that is not to say the question "Did he go to Cambridge yesterday?" hasn't got an answer.'

Williams is also unimpressed by arguments based on the idea of incommensurability – the impossibility of translating some or even all ideas from one language or conceptual system to another. 'That's true too,' concedes Williams. 'That doesn't mean that what people say in those vocabularies may not be absolutely, non-relatively true. It simply means that they are not inter-translatable. That's true too, not that that's any skin off my nose.'

Williams also denies, along with the deniers he attacks, the possibility of a 'super-assertable' account of society or history. He explains this idea in comparison to science.

'Scientists, or perhaps more so celebrators of science, talk about the truth about the universe. None of them, unless he's mad, thinks that there is one finite set of propositions which are all the true propositions about the universe. When they talk about the truth about the universe they mean the fundamental explanatory account of the universe which will give you all the laws of nature and all the basic concepts of science. Some scientists think it's reasonable to aim for such a thing, some just don't. If there were such a thing, I guess it would be what Crispin Wright calls "super-assertable": if you got it right nothing would ever come in to force you to change it. In that sense I don't believe that there is a truth about the past or about a given society. I think the aim that you should arrive at a historical account of how we got to where we are which is super-assertable is totally mistaken.'

This willingness to accept what the deniers have got right is essential to Williams' enterprise, for he believes that the problem about the debate between the deniers and their critics is 'that these parties largely pass each other by, because roughly the deniers have got some concerns which they wrongly express as a general worry about truth. The other guys are actually right about truth but don't realize there are a lot of problems about the things the deniers are worried about. So I try to say why the deniers are wrong but at the same time that doesn't mean we fall back on a kind of commonsensical positivism that just says history consists in lots of facts or something.'

Where Williams will not concede ground to the deniers, however, is in his insistence that to have a concern with truthfulness, sincerity and accuracy does require the concept of truth. 'Otherwise it's incoherent. Truthfulness presumably means, for Dick Rorty, or anybody else, roughly saying what you believe. I don't know how you're ever supposed to explain belief as one disposition or mental state among others without mentioning the truth. Not because all beliefs have to be true, but because their great characteristic, which in some sense needs to be explained, is that they aim at truth and also that falsehood is an objection to them. If I say, "I wonder whether such and such," and somebody says it isn't so, it's false, then I say, "Damn, oh well I just wondered." But if I say, "I believe, I'm firmly convinced that so and so," and they say, "Well, I'm going to show you you're false," I would do something about my belief. Now how can you explain belief without using the notion of truth?'

Williams explains the limits of his tolerance for the deniers with a typically telling anecdote. 'There's a famous remark I quote in the book. Some German diplomat said to French statesman Clemenceau at the treaty of Versailles, "I wonder what historians will make of this?" Clemenceau said, "They won't say Belgium invaded Germany." That is quite an observation, I think.'

Truth and Truthfulness is an ambitious work, and its journeys into history give it a breadth unusual in these days of increased academic specialization. Williams has earned the licence to be this ambitious, but isn't it a problem that it's more difficult for academics in general to do this kind of thing?

'Yes it is more difficult and yes it's a shame, and to some extent it's unavoidable,' he says, making it clear that 'specialization' is not entirely a bad thing. 'It's not just an organizational misunderstanding,' he explains. 'Philosophy is a specialized subject with specialized divisions. The division of labour applies to philosophy itself. The old idea of the sage who knows a bit of everything is pretty bogus actually and I'm rather against it. What I do think though is this: that while all that's true, it only gets worse if you adopt an attitude which says that it's not only bad luck that we don't have enough time and energy to know about other things, but that actually there's no need to, that's not the point.'

Williams is also unimpressed by the different attitudes shown towards scientific and other forms of knowledge, something he sees as tied up with the current 'scientism' of some philosophy. 'They don't seem to think it's improper to suppose that people can find time to learn some science. If they're coming into the philosophy of mind then these days they're quite often expected to know a bit about the relevant areas of perceptual psychology, developmental psychology, neurophysiology or whatever might be needed. If they can learn that, they can learn a certain amount of history.'

Removing these barriers to broader frames of reference for philosophers is a matter not so much of theory as of administration: 'A more relaxed or humanistic attitude on the part of people who are hiring in philosophy could help people in this respect.'

Williams' dislike of artificial boundaries extends to the so-called analytic/Continental divide, a distinction between two modes of philosophizing, the depth of which is being increasingly questioned.

'I'm not interested in the distinction between analytic and Continental philosophy, nor necessarily in being an analytic philosopher. I simply recognize that I will be regarded as one,' says Williams. But although he reluctantly accepts the label, he sees much that is wrong in the analytic world. 'What I do reject is the scientism of a lot of analytic philosophy now. I'm suspicious of the dignity it gives to a certain kind of very elaborate theory. I've always been a bit opposed to that, above all in ethics.'

He also has mixed feelings about the Continental tradition. 'Manifestly I'm not against "Continental" philosophy because the major inspiration for *Truth and Truthfulness* lies in Nietzsche, whom I take to be a "Continental" philosopher. That doesn't commit me to thinking that Derrida is a great thinker. I agree with those who rightly say that various "Continental" thinkers or thinkers esteemed by "Continental" philosophers are just as important or more important than quite a lot of 'analytic' philosophers. But they tend to have a weakness, which is they are over-impressed by the portentous in philosophy. In fact I think that was Heidegger's treachery to Nietzsche. Nietzsche removed the portentousness in philosophy. People think that's a joke because they think about

Zarathustra and all that, but in fact if you read most of Nietzsche, the one thing he never is is *professorially* portentous. He may be badly *poetically* portentous. Heidegger put the portentousness back into German philosophy and that is a terrible thing to have done, and a betrayal of Nietzsche.

'Analytic philosophy isn't too bad about that. The best strains realize correctly in my view the importance of the everyday or to cheer up "Continental" philosophers, the *alltëglich*. The idea that what you say just in the ordinary business of life is exceedingly important for one's understanding of these matters is very central.'

Williams' work seems to me to exhibit many of the virtues of Anglo-Saxon philosophy without its vices. In particular, he has a sensitivity to conceptual distinctions and to making the right ones, combined with a not so typical acceptance that you can't make too much of them, and that the world cannot be as neatly carved up as language can.

'Something can be over-distinguished or under-distinguished, that's true,' he agrees. 'The need for another distinction always has to show itself. You shouldn't do it just for the hell of it. It's because something won't work, you find that there's something which is being pulled in two directions at once so there must be something to be said about that.

'Another thing is that I think that there's a difference between a multiplication of distinctions being false, that it's actually representing a wrong view, and its being okay but simply irrelevant, useless – the machine has started to go on, on its own. I think that a lot of philosophy consists of that. I take the rough definition of scholasticism in its broader sense to be pursuing distinctions beyond a point at which they have anything to do which would worry any grown-up person about this kind of subject matter.'

This kind of failing is not confined to the abstract areas of philosophy. Indeed, Williams is most scornful of what he calls the 'applied ethics industry'.

'My feeling about it is that it contains one word, "applied", and another word, "ethics". For "applied", there's a machinery including the dreaded three kinds of ethical theory – Kantian, utilitarian, rights and whatever it may be – and you sort of move to the scene rather like the arrival of a forensic laboratory. It's all wheeled in and everything is carved up in terms of what "the utilitarian" or "the Kantian" would say. That involves a straitjacketing of the phenomenon.

'The second is "ethical", because in the nature of the case moral categories start trying to run the whole show. There's a lot to be learned from the experience of these things, in which you need to get under the skin of the people who are involved. I frankly find quite a lot of the literature about abortion or voluntary euthanasia or something of this kind, whether it's for or against, unappealing, because it seems to have some tremendously dogmatic view which isn't terribly close to what it's like to have a miscarriage or to have an abortion or to be in the dilemma of a caring person looking after another person who wants to die or whatever. There's a lot of preaching from both "liberals" and "conservatives". I don't think I have a recipe, but I don't think the machinery of applied ethics really helps.'

However, although his blood pressure seems to rise when talking about applied ethics, on the whole Williams is phlegmatic about the failure of much philosophy to make an impact. 'Ninety per cent of philosophy at any time is not much good. Ninety per cent of any subject is not much good. The difference with philosophy is that if it isn't much good it doesn't really add an awful lot, so it isn't clear why it's there. But there are two ways of not being much good: one is by being dry, boring and scholastic, and the other is by being bogus. I think philosophy mostly specializes in being dry and boring rather than being bogus. It's a matter of taste which you think is worse, and there's something to be said for the dry virtues of dry work against the emptiness of preposterous, pretentious work.'

Fortunately, in Williams' case, one doesn't have to choose between dryness and pretension, for both are refreshingly absent, in his work and himself.

Suggested Reading

Truth and Truthfulness: An Essay in Genealogy (Princeton University Press)
Philosophy as a Humanistic Discipline (Princeton University Press)

*   *   *   *   *

Afterword

When I interviewed Bernard Williams in the summer of 2002, I was aware that I had been granted a great privilege. An audience with a great thinker is always an honour and many believed Williams to be the finest British philosopher of his generation. But I was also aware that Williams had been ill, and only a few years before many would not have rated his chances of still being available for interview in 2002.

As it turned out, Williams appeared to be in rude health. He had the slightly shrivelled leanness of a man whose sickness had taken a lot out of him, but in conversation he had the energy and sharpness that belied his 72 years and recent travails.

But one year later he was to die. During those twelve months he published his swan song, *Truth and Truthfulness,* and saw it received with a warmth that reflected not only that volume's many merits, but also a kind of collective wish to honour a lifetime of achievement. Williams went out on a high note.

The interview I conducted with him contained much which had to be omitted from the first printed version. As a tribute to Williams, some of those unpublished exchanges are presented here, testimony to the subtlety and range of Williams' philosophy.

Philosophy in public life

Bernard Williams was active in public life, sitting on or chairing various committees. In the late 1970s, for example, he chaired a government committee on film censorship. How much philosophy did he bring to these endeavours?

'Oh quite a lot of philosophy in that particular case. As you know I've been on various other committees and much less philosophy went into others. For instance, I was a member of a royal commission on gambling and for that I had to learn enough about roulette to work out what the house's odds were, that kind of thing. That wasn't very philosophical.

'The film censorship committee was quite an interesting case because the reason why it was philosophical was not because it was applied philosophy in a moral theory sense. I did invoke the famous harm principle and I also said there was a right to free speech – I didn't elaborate on that, because I didn't think the report was the right place for a lot of metaethics.

'One thing one has to remember is that one is writing a document which is the proposal for a law in a given legislature. That's a very important fact. If that report had been written in the United States it couldn't have been written like that. It would have to have started from the First Amendment, because the First Amendment is the structure in which that law, by reason of the constitution of the United States, is discussed, which it isn't in England.

'The censorship report involves philosophy in various ways. It separates the issues that are involved in freedom of speech: does it involve no suppression at all? Can you have things that are restricted but not forbidden? Things of that sort. It involves issues about what the alleged offensive material is, which is why it contains discriminations which as far as I know don't occur anywhere else, about being obscene, offensive, pornographic, exploitative and so on. There's less on being exploitative than there would have been had it been written later. It would have had to have been quite a different dimension of discourse relating to some of the things MacKinnon and more recently Rae Langton have said and so on.

'It also has some speculations in a way about the philosophy of aesthetic experience, about the nature of the relations between the pornographic and the erotic. I thought that was actually one of the more important philosophical contributions.

'Let's put it this way: I think a philosophical training has got to help in getting together this sort of argument.'

Defending the Enlightenment

Bernard Williams had always displayed a willingness to defend the indefensible and attack the unassailable, though often in unpredictable ways, which wrong-footed opponents. Such is his defence of the ideals of the Enlightenment.

'I think it's fashionable to debunk the Enlightenment and certain claims, it seems to me, are not only absolutely wrong but ludicrous,' he says. 'The idea advocated by Horkheimer and Adorno in the *Dialectic of Enlightenment* – which is roughly that the Enlightenment of the *Encylopédie* and the eighteenth century and all that is responsible for Auschwitz – is breathtaking.'

But Williams wouldn't be Williams if he didn't at the same time acknowledge the 'mite of truth' in the position he is attacking.

'There is an aspect of the Enlightenment which identified social understanding with theoretical understanding, whose picture of society was fundamentally externalized and which had a concept of rational efficiency. I find the largest embodiment of that in Bentham's kind of mechanized utilitarianism. I do think that's dangerous. I've written elsewhere against utilitarianism and I think it's terrible for society.

'On the other hand, there's an aspect of Enlightenment as critique, which was embodied above all in figures such as Diderot. That aspect of critique seems to me to have great validity and I think in a negative way it does underpin some liberal views, because it gives us a more minimalist support for political practices than you get out of theocratic, hierarchical opinions.'

What philosophers do

To put it rather crudely, there are those who see philosophy's role to be about attaining a greater clarity and those who see it as aiming at some kind of certainty. In other words, it is the difference between those who think philosophy is to do with getting a deeper understanding and those who think that it's about arriving at solutions. Does Williams agree that he belongs more to the first camp?

'Absolutely. I think there are puzzles and some of these puzzles are very interesting and some of them are soluble as puzzles. One mustn't underestimate the extent to which in a large number of areas philosophy does simply "make progress".

'I think that philosophy is the product of our realizing that we don't understand what we're doing, above all in describing the world, finding out about it, trying to act in it. We simply don't realize that we don't understand our own world, we don't understand what we're up to. That requires us to reflect on the concepts that we use. And I think philosophy can be defined as conceptual reflection as long as that doesn't have any of three implications often associated with it.

'It doesn't mean first of all that it's all ruthlessly second-order. [About how we know rather than what we know.] In some areas, the philosophy of mind and so on, people need to learn about scientific discoveries to learn what we're up to. Secondly it doesn't imply that philosophy doesn't involve history, because we can't understand some of our concepts at all unless we understand their history. Thirdly, it doesn't mean that it can't be revisionary or denunciatory because what we may come to understand is that what we're doing with our concepts is engaging in some mystification, ideological imposition or straight confusion.

'This is all opposed to the traditional views of "linguistic philosophy" which is first of all that it's all about language, it was all second-order; second that it was pure, it had to be distinguished from science, history or anything else; third, that it was fundamentally descriptive, conservative. I reject all of that.'

Williams belongs to a generation of philosophers, many of whom have been criticized for producing a kind of philosophy which is dry, remote and parochial. Does he think there is anything to those criticisms?

'I don't think they're altogether misplaced, but I do think that they're misplaced as particularly applying to this generation. The thing is that I myself have gone in for some of this, namely in my attacks on "academic moral philosophy" which I think is substantially, in various ways, a useless enterprise. That has nothing particularly to do with my generation. The moral theorists are worse at it now than they were before. Some of them, not all of them by any means, elaborate one piece of theoretical nonsense or other.'

Williams is also wary of the general tendency of philosophers to criticize those branches of the subject that are not their own.

'I found, rather ironically in *New British Philosophy: The Interviews*, that when people attack subjects as being empty of any general significance or "purely academic", it's usually somebody else's subject. For example, somebody near the beginning of that book tells somebody off for doing some subject which if done well might be quite interesting. Then later in the book we find people discussing vagueness, we find them discussing sense data, for God's sake. If somebody wanted to find that boring they could equally do so. The fact is it isn't about the subject matter. It's about whether what is done is interesting and lively and creative or whether it's purely scholastic.'

Williams on Diderot and Voltaire

'Diderot's my Enlightenment hero, much more than Voltaire, who I think was a mildly despotic and unpleasing individual, vastly overestimated in his influence. It's puzzling that Russell made such a fuss about Voltaire. I think Voltaire's a terrible man, but I think Diderot's a marvellous figure.'

Williams on J. L. Austin

'Austin's work was very radical. He did the same as Wittgenstein in a very different style, namely he rejected many of the categories of philosophical importance. I don't personally think that Austin lived long enough to ever find a way to harness his kind of linguistic enquiry onto anything that you could call a set of philosophical problems, except sometimes. I don't think he had a general method. What I do think is that he was actually rather radical and that was what some people didn't like.

'Austin had a curiously English characteristic of playing up the kind of grammar-school master aspect of his personality. In the 1950s, when Austin went to Berkeley, Stanley Cavell was absolutely taken with him. He thought he was wonderful, a kind of extraordinary exotic animal and drew great inspiration from him, some of it I think very interesting. The trouble is that I recognized Austin only too well, because I'd been to an English grammar school. He was the Latin master who told you off for not having got your subject correct.'

Robert M. Pirsig

What is the most important work of philosophy to be written in the last 50 years? Ask a panel of experts and you'll probably be told it's something like Rawls' *Theory of Justice*, MacIntyre's *After Virtue*, or Kuhn's *The Structure of Scientific Revolutions* – none of which will be known to the average person in the street. Jo Public, though, is perhaps most likely to mention an international bestseller: *Zen and the Art of Motorcycle Maintenance: An Inquiry Into Values* by Robert M. Pirsig, published in 1974.

Our panel of experts would quickly dismiss this nomination. Pirsig's impact on professional philosophy has been negligible. His big idea is what he calls the Metaphysics of Quality (or MOQ). This constitutes 'a philosophic answer to the question of what is Quality, or worth, or merit, or value, or betterness or any of the other synonyms for good. There are many possible answers, but the one the MOQ gives is that you can understand Quality best if you don't subordinate it to anything else but instead subordinate everything else to it.

'It says there are two basic kinds of Quality, an undefined Quality called Dynamic Quality, and a defined Quality called Static Quality. Static Quality is further divided into four evolutionary divisions: inorganic, biological, social and intellectual. Our entire understanding of the world can be organized within this framework. When you do so things fall into place that were poorly defined before, and new things appear that were concealed under previous frameworks of understanding. The MOQ is not intended to deny previous modes of understanding as much as to expand them into a more inclusive picture of what it's all about.'

Whatever one makes of this, it just is the case that it remains almost entirely undiscussed and unstudied in university philosophy departments. Only one PhD has ever been awarded for a thesis on Pirsig's ideas, to Anthony McWatt at Liverpool University in 2005. McWatt also organized what he billed as the first academic philosophy conference on the Metaphysics of Quality. But even this turns out to be only a half-step into academe for Pirsig: when I asked about how a spoof paper was accepted into the programme, McWatt told me the conference had been 'arranged at the last minute on an ad hoc basis' and that 'anyone invited to the conference was free to present a paper of whatever viewpoint they wanted'. So not what would usually be deemed an academic conference.

But then Pirsig is used to being an outsider. The *Guinness Book of Records* lists *Zen and the Art of Motorcycle Maintenance* as the bestseller that was rejected by the largest number of publishers: 121. Yet as the book became a hit, recognition seemed to be his at last. *Zen* combined a fictionalized, autobiographical account of a motorcycle journey with philosophical discourses, or 'chautauquas'. It received glowing reviews from highly respected sources. The *New York Review of Books* said 'Pirsig is a stunning writer of fictional prose', the *New York Times* declared it to be 'profoundly important', and the *Sunday Times* called it 'an astonishing literary performance'. George Steiner would later compare Pirsig's writing to Dostoevsky, Proust and Bergson.

Pirsig was awarded a Guggenheim Fellowship to write the sequel, *Lila: An Inquiry Into Morals* (1991). 'While *Zen and the Art of Motorcycle Maintenance* is a skeleton of a philosophy enclosed within a full-bodied novel,' Pirsig told me, '*Lila* is a skeleton of a novel enclosed within a full-bodied philosophy.' Lila developed the Metaphysics of Quality more fully, but despite receiving several good reviews and spending six weeks on the *New York Times* bestseller list, it failed to attract the interest of academe and lacked the enduring appeal of *Zen*.

Since then, Pirsig has published virtually nothing and rarely talked publicly. So when I was offered the opportunity of an exclusive interview with him, the offer was irresistible. There was, however, a catch: the interview would be by email. Obviously this is not ideal. An email interview removes a lot of the spontaneity and cut-and-thrust of a face-to-face conversation. However, Pirsig is such an exceptional figure, it was decided to go ahead anyway.

In retrospect, perhaps this was the wrong decision. The exchange often seemed not to connect, and perhaps the medium in which it took place was a major factor. By the end, Pirsig himself was clearly disappointed with the result, writing: 'We have come to a standoff here, where I have refused to talk about what other philosophers are saying, and you have neglected to ask underlying questions about what I am saying. What is most remarkable to me about this interview is that not a single question has been asked about what the Metaphysics of Quality actually says. You say there is more to philosophy than I know, and that is no doubt true. I have a degree in philosophy and know quite well that no one knows it all. But there is more to the Metaphysics of Quality than you have shown any indication of understanding, and there was an opportunity to find out more that has been missed. In journalism, where I hold an MA, it is mandatory that when you interview someone you try sincerely to understand what they are saying, not just try to impose other people's views on them, including your own.'

It is possible for you to make up your own mind as to whether this is fair by reading the entire transcript of our exchange online (www.philosophersnet.com/magazine/pirsig_transcript.htm). Whatever your verdict, Pirsig's complaint reflects a tension that ran through the interview. Pirsig wanted to talk about his philosophy and his philosophy alone. I wanted to relate that philosophy to the ideas of others, as a means of bringing out what is supposedly different or superior in it, and also as a means of questioning it. After all, if the purpose were just to reiterate what Pirsig has already said, we should simply tell people to read his books, or just invite him to provide an overview of his philosophy.

So, for instance, I began by asking, 'There are all sorts of echoes and references to the mainstream philosophical tradition in your books, yet it is not obvious where or how you fit into that tradition. You have, for example, been referred to as an American pragmatist philosopher. Where would you locate your work in the history of philosophy?'

'The Metaphysics of Quality is not intended to be within any philosophic tradition,' he replied, 'although obviously it was not written in a vacuum. My first awareness that it resembled James' work came from a magazine review long after *Zen and the Art of Motorcycle Maintenance* was published. The Metaphysics of Quality's central idea that the world is nothing but value is not part of any philosophic tradition that I know of. I have proposed it because it seems to me that when you look into it carefully it makes more sense than all the other things the world is supposed to be composed of.'

Much as I appreciate Pirsig's desire not to be labelled according to the standard, extant divisions in philosophy, there is surely something of a tension in this kind of reply. On the one hand, he is not interested in relating his ideas to those of others, but on the other he is claiming that his theory makes more sense than all others. But to make the latter claim persuasively, I think you have to engage with those competing ideas, which is something Pirsig seemed reluctant to do.

Furthermore, when he does criticize the ideas of others, his dismissal of them often seems perfunctory. For example, in *Lila* he wrote '[The theory of evolution] goes into many volumes about how the fittest survive but never once goes into the question of why.'

I put it to him that most biologists would see that as blatantly untrue, and that furthermore, if he thinks the question of why the fittest survive hasn't been answered by the theory of evolution, he just hasn't understood it.

'I would answer that biologists who think my question doesn't understand the theory of evolution are biologists who do not understand the difference between "how" and "why"', he replied. 'The answers they give for "why" are usually "competitive advantage" or "survival of the fittest". But if you look closely you will see that these are not scientific terms. "Fittest" is a subjective term. It exists only in the mind of a scientific observer. It isn't out there in the nature he observes. The same is true of "advantage". Ask a biologist who thinks my question doesn't understand the theory of evolution, to define in exact scientific terms the meaning of these evaluative words. If he takes time to do so, I predict he will give up or he will come up with nonsense or he will find himself drifting eventually toward the solutions arrived at by the Metaphysics of Quality.'

The problem with this reply is that though 'fittest' may appear to be an evaluative term, for evolutionists it is no such thing, but simply describes how well an organism and its relatives are able to survive in the environment in which they find themselves.

In a similar vein, I try to explore the apparent parallels between Pirsig's philosophy and other philosophies that are committed to metaphysical monism, such as that of Spinoza. I put it to him that the Metaphysics of Quality shares with these predecessors an attempt to dissolve the puzzle that the world seems to contain many things that are real yet seemingly incommensurable – such as mind and matter, fact and value, objectivity and subjectivity – by arguing that these are all just aspects of one, unified thing. Given that Pirsig claims his metaphysics is a Copernican revolution on a par with Kant's, doesn't the existence of these precursors rather deflate that claim?

Pirsig answered, 'I may have read Spinoza incorrectly but it has seemed to me that his assertion that God is the fundamental constituent of the Universe was not very revolutionary, given the church attitudes at the time.'

To say that Spinoza's views were not very revolutionary seemed to me an extraordinary claim, since the impersonal 'god-or-nature' he postulated was entirely different from that of the Jewish or Christian religion.

Pirsig simply replied, 'If the claim seems extraordinary to you, then I withdraw it. I am not a "Spinozist" and made it clear that I may have read him incorrectly.' But if you are going to claim great originality for your theories, surely you should make sure they really are original?

Despite Pirsig's later claim that I showed no interest in understanding his metaphysics, we did discuss several aspects of it, including the exact nature of 'Quality', and its role in his philosophy. However, he resisted my attempt to relate this to the traditional philosophical concepts of monism and dualism, which categorize theories in terms of the number of basic substances they claim exist – one or two, respectively.

'You are correct in saying that the revolutionary assertion of the Metaphysics of Quality is that "Quality" or "value" is the fundamental constituent of the universe,' he wrote. 'However, the classification of metaphysics into monism, dualism and pluralism, seems to me to be an arbitrary classification where none is needed. The Metaphysics of Quality is all three: Quality is the monism. Static Quality and Dynamic Quality are the dualism, and the four levels of static quality contain a pluralism of things.'

But why is the classification of metaphysics into monism, dualism and pluralism arbitrary?

'I think it is arbitrary in the way a count of the length of sentences in a metaphysics would be arbitrary. It doesn't add anything to the truth or falsehood of the metaphysics being described. It is a form of philosophology, if I may use a favourite word, a classification of philosophy rather than philosophy itself.'

I'm not convinced. Of course, I continued, many systems have pairs, trios, quartets (and so forth) of concepts. But it seems perfectly reasonable to classify metaphysical systems as monist or dualist on the basis of how many basic substances they believe the universe most fundamentally comprises.

'The "Quality" of the Metaphysics of Quality is not a basic substance, or anything like it. The Buddhists call it "nothingness" precisely to avoid that kind of intellectual characterization. Once you start to define Quality as a basic substance you are off on a completely different path from the Metaphysics of Quality.'

I'm left somewhat confused by the fact that 'quality' or 'value' is the 'fundamental constituent of the universe', but that 'The "Quality" of the Metaphysics of Quality is not a basic substance, or anything like it.' Given that 'substance' in the broad sense is usually understood to mean the constituent of whatever exists, and is not taken to refer solely to physical matter, could Pirsig explain further how quality is a basic constituent but not a substance?

'I'm not original on this point,' he replies, 'except to identify Quality with the Tao and with Buddha-nature (hence the title of *Zen and the Art of Motorcycle Maintenance*). The amount of material on these two would overflow most library rooms, but it is essential to both that the basic constituent of the universe is nothingness, and by this is meant not empty space but "no-thingness". It is somewhat incorrect to call "no-thingness" a basic constituent since it is not really even that (it is not even an it), but in an everyday philosophic "finger-pointing-toward-the-moon" discourse that's about as good as you can get. It is very incorrect to call it a substance in the way that substance is usually meant today.'

I think these answers again show some difficulties of our interview. Pirsig often replies by either pointing to a huge stack of literature elsewhere, or by appealing to the essential indefinablity of key terms. For instance, when I ask, sceptically, about the apparent lack of arguments underpinning the Metaphysics of Quality, he replies, 'I and many others think that these arguments are in fact contained in *Zen and the Art of Motorcycle Maintenance* and *Lila*. I do not know of any philosophical system that leaves all questions answered to everyone's satisfaction in one volume. The MOQ.org website since 1997 has averaged about 500 posts per month, containing arguments for and against the Metaphysics of Quality. That comes to 42,000 posts. That's a lot of arguments. There is an entire book called *Lila's Child* that is extracted from these arguments, with annotations by myself.'

As to his replies gesturing towards the essential indefinability of things, he uses the metaphor that the Metaphysics of Quality is 'just another finger pointing toward the moon'. What would he say to the suggestion that we should take that comment perhaps more literally than he intended and say that all his talk of Quality and value should be seen merely as useful ways of seeing things, and we shouldn't worry about whether it is literally true? Should we just see metaphysics as metaphor?

'I think that we should see metaphysics as metaphor to the extent that metaphor is literally true,' he says, gnomically. In my analytic literal-mindedness, I don't accept that as a clear enough answer. In what sense can a metaphor be literally true? We normally understand metaphor in contrast to literal truth. 'The sun is shining' is literally true; 'The sun is shining in my heart' is metaphorically true. Whether metaphysics deals in statements of the first or second kind seems to me an important question.

'I am really not familiar with the question but seem to remember reading that if the "mythos-over-logos" line of thought is followed, then metaphors are literally true since all our knowledge, including scientific knowledge, is metaphorical. In a subject–object metaphysics, metaphors are clearly subjective and literal truth is clearly objective. But if the foundations of the subject–object metaphysics are rejected then the question of whether metaphysics is metaphor or literal truth goes out the window with it. It becomes moot.'

My suspicion is that Pirsig's frustration with me is rooted in his deep-seated conviction that his theory is right and to do anything other than explain it is a pointless distraction. And relating it to what others have had to say is the most pointless distraction of all. It is as though he thinks the Metaphysics of Quality is self-evidently true to anyone who takes the trouble to understand it properly. It needs no further support. He says that the reason for accepting Quality as the fundamental constituent of the universe is that 'We gain a far better way of organizing our understanding of everything, from physics to religion. That gain is its own justification.' Indeed, the beauty of the metaphysical construct seems sufficient reason to embrace it: 'I think the Metaphysics of Quality would say that true ideas are more beautiful than false ones,' he says.

I do have some sympathy for Pirsig's distaste for how academic philosophy encourages an inward-looking conservatism that makes it resistant to genuinely new ideas: '[Philosophers], instead of coming to grips with the philosophy at hand, sometimes dismiss it by saying, "Oh he is saying the same as someone else," or "Someone else has said it much better." This is the latter half of the well-known conservative argument that some new idea is (a) no good because it hasn't been heard before or (b) it is no good because it has been heard before. If, as has been noted by R. C. Zaehner, once the Oxford University Professor of Eastern Religions and Ethics, I am saying the same thing as Aristotle; and if, as has been noted in the *Harvard Educational Review*, I am saying the same thing as William James; and if, as has been noted now, I may be saying the same thing as Spinoza: then why has no one ever noticed that Aristotle and Spinoza and William James are all saying the same thing? This kind of commentary has a parallel in literary criticism where various authors are compared to one another in an easy way without any serious attempt to fathom what any of them are really saying. So, if Hemingway says death is a terrible thing, why then Hemingway is saying the same thing as Shakespeare! What a discovery! And Shakespeare has said it so much better. Who needs to read Hemingway?'

Pirsig has coined the term 'philosophology' to contrast with real philosophy. The distinction parallels that between literary critics and writers. Philosophologists write about the philosophy of others and philosophers actually write their own philosophy. I tell Pirsig that I agree that one of the main trappings of academic philosophy is that it encourages the former rather than the latter. He accepts that 'most philosophologists also philosophize and most philosophers also philosophologize', but I suggest that the good reason many philosophers spend a lot of time discussing the ideas of other philosophers is because they appreciate that the ideas they have do not emerge out of a vacuum, but have been shaped and preceded by the ideas of many great thinkers. Further, by constantly thinking about how their ideas relate and compare to those of their peers and the greats of the past, they hope to learn from them, and not to repeat errors.

'The division between authors and literary critics throws light on this subject,' says Pirsig. 'The author is a creator and the critic is a judge. Literary critics normally do not pretend they are authors when they judge a book, but philosophologists do pretend they are philosophers when they judge someone else's philosophy. The best of literary critics know that an author has to work alone and not go around showing his manuscript to everybody, because his source is not what everyone else has said. He has to be out there finding things where nobody has gone before. Because philosophologists think of themselves as philosophers, they do not understand that a real philosopher is not doing the same thing they are, and should not be doing the same thing they are if he wants to come up with genuine philosophy, and not just more of the usual repetition and dissection of old ideas.'

As our exchange drew to a close, I wanted to make my own unease explicit. So in my final question I outlined my own personal response to Pirsig, and asked what he made of it.

'I think both books reveal an author of exceptional intelligence and insight,' I wrote. 'However, I do feel that in seeking to build an all-encompassing system to connect all these insights, we end up with a whole which is less than the sum of its parts. Perhaps this does little more than reflect the extent to which my own thinking has been affected (or infected) with the anti-metaphysical bias of recent Anglo-American philosophy. But I don't think it is just that. I think rather that it connects to the above point about philosophology. You have not allowed yourself to be constrained by other philosophers, which has given you the benefit of more freedom and more originality. But constraints also provide checks and balances, and without them, I fear you've constructed a system on foundations that are not up to the job of supporting it.'

'The foundations are okay, in fact they are rock-solid, but we never got to discuss them,' he replied. He then went on to make the comments included earlier about how our interview had resulted in a standoff. But we had discussed where the arguments to support the Metaphysics of Quality were to be found, why we should accept it, its relation to the subject–object distinction (which space has not allowed me to include here), whether it was metaphorically or literally true, what was revolutionary about it, whether it was a monist theory and so on.

It seems to me that Pirsig's dissatisfaction has deeper roots than this, and perhaps the experience of this interview will help dig them up. Pirsig desires contradictory things. He wants to be seen as an original thinker, not constrained by the philosophy of his predecessors; but he also wants to be recognized by the very people whose whole understanding of philosophy is based on those predecessors, and who justifiably believe that newcomers must be judged at least in part by how they measure up to them.

'[It] does bother me that *Lila* is not as successful as it should be among academic philosophers,' he told me early in our exchange. 'In my opinion it's a much more important book than *Zen and the Art of Motorcycle Maintenance*. My feeling is like that of someone trying to sell five-dollar bills for two dollars apiece and hardly making a sale. Readers of *Lila* are naturally leery because they're not used to the idea of a Metaphysics of Quality, but I think that if they eventually understand what is being offered, there will be a change of mind. Perhaps these questions in *The Philosophers' Magazine* mark a beginning. After all these years I'm grateful to hear them stated openly.'

By the end, I wonder if his gratitude to my series of sceptical questions remained. I am sure he is disappointed that I turned out to be too like the 'philosophologists' he decries. But perhaps a true outsider has to remain without. I'm sure that nothing I asked him will cause him to doubt for one minute the truth of his philosophy. But it might just confirm his suspicion that engaging with the philosophical mainstream is a waste of time. Like our interview, neither side is prepared to engage on the other's terms, but both sides believe they have excellent reasons for standing their ground. Would face-to-face discussion overcome this? Perhaps. But in the meantime we remain with what Pirsig rightly called a standoff, but one which cannot be blamed on one party alone, and which currently seems to suit the establishment more than it does Pirsig.

Suggested Reading

Zen and the Art of Motorcycle Maintenance: An Inquiry into Values (Harper
     Torch)
Lila: An Inquiry into Morals (Alma Books)

14 Philosophy and the Novel
Alexander McCall Smith

Alexander McCall Smith is probably best known as the author of the hugely popular *No. 1 Ladies' Detective Agency* novels, which tell the story of Precious Ramotswe, the first woman detective in Botswana, and the detective agency, based in Gaborone, that she founded. However, what is less well known is that he is also Emeritus Professor of Medical Law at Edinburgh University, and has a CV which suggests he has as much claim to the label of philosopher as anyone.

McCall Smith has written over 50 books, many of them philosophical in nature. With Ken Mason, he wrote the classic textbook, *Law and Medical Ethics*, which is now in its sixth edition. With Michael Menlowe he wrote *The Duty to Rescue*, in which he examined 'the boundaries of moral obligation and the extent to which we have a duty to act'. And while a visiting professor at Dullas University, he wrote *Justice and the Prosecution of Old Crimes*, with Dan Shuman.

In addition to all this, he was on the international bioethics commission of UNESCO, has been the vice-chairman of the Human Genetics Commission, and has chaired the new *British Medical Journal*'s ethics committee. So much for being a non-philosopher.

McCall Smith's engagement with philosophy goes back a long way. 'I first came into contact with philosophy at university when I was studying jurisprudence, which I was particularly keen on,' he told me over coffee. 'The way in which jurisprudence was taught at that particular time was as a branch of philosophy. So we looked at theories of law, issues of the individual and the state, and natural law, of course, which took one into fairly mainstream philosophy. I found all this quite interesting and, indeed, as an undergraduate, I did a specialist course in which I spent a lot of time thinking about natural law. It was this that led me to become a little bit more interested in, not just philosophy, but other branches of philosophy.'

The interest was maintained when McCall Smith started to work in the area of criminal law. 'My PhD thesis was actually part criminal law, part philosophy. I was looking at the concept of coercion. That led me to read a lot about freedom of action, studies of intention and theories of action in general.' And though his professional life would take further turns, it seems philosophy always turned with him. 'Then my career rather went into the area of medical law and medical ethics, so I became very interested at that stage and still continue to have an interest in what I suppose we might loosely call applied ethics. Medical law is a remarkably broad church, because it includes not only very specifically legal issues, but also major moral questions associated with issues of life and death: all the usual ones, euthanasia, definitions of death, issues of responsibility for omissions. So a lot of my time I was actually reading the philosophical literature rather than the specifically legal literature.'

It should not therefore be surprising to find that he has chosen a philosopher as the protagonist in his new series of novels, *The Sunday Philosophy Club*. Isabel Dalhousie is the editor of the fictitious *Review of Applied Ethics* and an accidental amateur sleuth. It might surprise some to find that although this is very much a popular entertainment, the first novel of the series is packed with a lot of real philosophy. It's not just that Peter Strawson's 'Freedom and Resentment' and Sissela Bok's *Lying* both crop up quite naturally. It's also that the book, without ever coming across as ponderous or didactic, is very much concerned with everyday ethics and the importance of character to morality.

'I'm very interested in moral education. The development of moral imagination I think is absolutely crucial, but I'm also interested in how the building blocks of moral behaviour evolve through learning the moral habits of the heart and the inculcation of automatic responses. That ties in with my particular view of human action. I think that a lot of human action actually is much more automatic than we give it credit for. That's one of the things that interests me in the criminal context. I think a lot of the things that people do, a lot of the acts which they perform, are not necessarily the result of deliberation. There's brain injury work that indicates that we decide to act before we're conscious of the fact, or before we're actually even aware of the situations we confront. So I think some things as simple and old-fashioned as civility and manners really play very important functions, much more important than we would imagine, because they indicate a moral awareness of the other.'

Although, like most novelists (Paul Auster excepted), McCall Smith is keen to distinguish himself from his characters, Dalhousie's ruminations reflect his own 'considerable sympathy' for virtue ethics: the idea that the formation of character and the cultivation of virtues are crucial to morality.

'I'm very sympathetic to character theories of responsibility. Interestingly enough, if you look at early Scots criminal law and, for example, someone like Hume (not your Hume, but the criminal lawyer), there are whiffs of character theories. They talk about something called *dole* which they describe as a corrupt and malevolent cast of mind. Usually, criminal law is very concerned with what we call the *mens rea*, the mental state associated with a particular act. You could argue that a much more sophisticated theory of responsibility would look at the overall conduct of an individual which would go more towards character rather than taking an individual, terribly isolated snapshot.'

Many of McCall Smith's other philosophical interests find their way into the novel. For instance, his characters struggle with *akrasia*, or weakness of will, a philosophical problem which has been discussed since Plato.

'I think the problem of akratic action – knowing how we should behave if we pay attention to the dictates of reason, and how we actually manage to behave – is one of the most difficult moral problems that we face in our lives. Most people struggle with that, and I think you can find many examples of that struggle in day-to-day life. For example, people know that they should be tolerant of others, so they probably know that they shouldn't be homophobic. But most people probably are. This leads to a great tension.'

It's a tension most evident when temptation is strong. 'Again, this is something people obviously encounter in their day-to-day life. Who doesn't encounter temptation of one sort or another, whether it's chocolate or sex?'

McCall Smith clearly relished his philosophy, and the number of issues he describes as 'strong interests' over the course of our conversation reveals both a breadth and depth of learning. Is there some sense in which, without being didactic, he wants to bring philosophy to the attention of more readers?

'Yes, I think so,' he replies, 'because I think readers of novels are very interested in it, and I think they probably don't get enough of it, because the novel has become very naturalistic. You get descriptions of people getting up and having their breakfast, brushing their teeth and so on in great detail, and maybe their emotions are looked at. But there's a bit of people's lives which is very concerned with how we should act and how we should live, which I think people are very seriously interested in. For example, look at how newspapers are bringing in these ethics columns, look at the way in which people have allegedly abandoned psychoanalysts for philosophers – for philosophical counsellors.

'So I do think there is real interest in these issues, and that people like talking about them. Certainly this is the feedback that I've had from readers in relation to the Ramotswe novels. Ramotswe is not a philosopher, but nonetheless she does talk about things like forgiveness and she does come up with fairly folksy observations, and readers are interested in thinking about these things.'

One way in which fiction can be an effective way of examining philosophical arguments is that it allows an exploration of the intersection of theory and practice, something that McCall Smith became acutely aware of in his work in practical medical ethics.

'There's a very practical, applied dimension, when you have to make a decision, and the policy implications and what is politically possible all have to be taken into account. That process – the conversation that you have with other people who are perhaps geneticists, doctors, genetic counsellors or whatever – is going to be very different from the discussion that you would have about a purely theoretical issue. And yet I don't think that the distinction is as sharp as some people would say. I'll give you an example.

'Some years ago I'd been asked to become involved in a New Zealand medical campaign to change the law relating to negligent homicide, which was being used to prosecute doctors who had lost patients in the course of medical treatment. It was a really extraordinary situation. I accepted, and I met Alan Merry, a professor of anaesthesia in New Zealand, and we discovered that he had a very strong interest in dealing at a practical level with the consequences of mistakes in practice, such as errors made in the application of complex procedures and drug doses. I had a very strong theoretical interest in the concept of negligence, how we actually define negligent conduct, and how you draw the boundaries of culpability around human action. For example, is negligent conduct ever going to be truly culpable, or do you actually have to be reckless before you can be held morally to blame? It seemed to me that the language all around us was quite confused and indeed that it was sometimes abused.

'I was interested in getting at how we define the accidental and the nature of accident, and interestingly enough there's very little philosophical literature on that particular issue. We use the word "accident" in a very loose sense. An accident might just be an unexpected, untoward event, which has no human culpability involved; or it could be the result of somebody driving too fast in a very clearly controlled speed zone. So even the language was vague, woolly and used incorrectly by people.

'So we sat down and thought "we're going to write a book on it", and it was the most wonderful thing to do. We both enjoyed it very much indeed. We there went into some of the very basic theoretical issues about the distinction between the accidental and the non-accidental, about what we mean when somebody is said to be behaving in a negligent fashion, about how we actually analyse faulty action in terms of the making of errors, and so on. All of this stuff was one of the most interesting things I've ever done. But the theoretical and practical were totally and completely integrated.'

Indeed, when we moved on to discuss what makes a good philosopher, this ability to bring the theoretical and the practical together was central to the answer he gave in response to my suggestion that something hard to define, call it insight, is essential for good philosophy.

'What is that insight? Is it an ability to place theoretical constructs in context, to moderate them with a sense of what actually will work or can work in human society? You could do philosophy in a very abstract way and reach conclusions which would be wrong, because they wouldn't accord with the real world which they're meant to be regulating. I mentioned earlier our work on mistakes and accidents, and if you look at the Continental criminal justice systems, they're much more theoretical. With the Continental code approach, they reach the conclusion that the concept of negligence should for theoretical reasons be the same in civil and criminal contexts. When you implement that, it leads to extremely harsh results. That's an example of where you've done all the theoretical work and have all these juridical concepts that should make sense, but they just don't apply to the world of ordinary affairs, for example, in medical practice where doctors are making immediate and emergency decisions. You can't be that harsh in judging human error, because then you're into psychology – you need psychological insights into how we make mistakes before we can talk about blame. If you merely study it as an isolated moral area, simply as a theoretical notion, then it is possible that you will come up with conclusions that are absolutely absurd, and which, as well as not working, would be extremely unjust.'

This is one reason why many otherwise great philosophers have fallen down when they have ventured into the world of public affairs. I wondered if Betrand Russell was one such example.

'Indeed, and there have been other philosophers whose political sense has been bizarre. One thinks of Sartre and some of the French philosophers' enthusiasm for Mao Tse-Tung. People who have had experience of the world will always recognize a tyrant.'

This element of common sense is a counterpoint to the intellectualizing which is more evident in the *No. 1 Ladies' Detective Agency* novels than in the new *Sunday Philosophy Club*.

'We shouldn't underestimate the importance and insights of people who have developed a sort of practical wisdom based on their experience. They may not have had the benefit of a philosophical education or much education at all, and yet some of them have a very profound idea of human conduct and nature. I would say that practical experience is of immense importance in developing a mature and defensible view of the world, and that somebody could read philosophy all day and never actually be able to deal with the world of human affairs.'

This connects with McCall Smith's respect for virtue ethics, which since Aristotle has seen philosophical analysis of ethics and the development of moral character as two distinct processes. For this reason, life experience or fiction may be more helpful to moral development than philosophy.

'I would have thought encouraging children to read works of fiction is one of the great ways of developing the faculty of moral imagination,' he says. 'You read about and enter into the world of others and develop your moral imagination. It's through stories that we develop our sense of the way the world works.'

Philosophy, however, remains important and will continue to feature in his forthcoming novels.

'The next book in the *Sunday Philosophy Club* series is going to deal with the ethics of memory as one of its themes, which I suppose is connected a little bit with this idea of the passage of time and guilt, which Dan Shuman and I explored in *Justice and the Prosecution of Old Crimes*.'

This is good news for those of us who want to see more philosophy out there, for in many ways the adventures of Isabel Dalhousie are better vehicles for popularizing philosophy than many more overtly introductory and popular books. The endorsement is mutual: 'It would be great if the readers thought "Oh well, I should go and read, well, *The Philosophers' Magazine*". I do think that the propagation of serious philosophical discussion is a great good.'

It's also been something he has greatly enjoyed. McCall Smith has more and finer strings on his bow than most of us can dream of, and he appreciates his good fortune.

'I've been very lucky in that I've had my professional place in the area of bioethics, medical policy and so on; and then I've been able to look out into other areas of philosophy. That's been a great pleasure and privilege for me to do, and now I'm doing a similar thing in bringing bits and pieces into fiction. So that's my role, in a way, and that's good. I enjoy it greatly.'

Suggested Reading

The Sunday Philosophy Club series is published in the UK by Little, Brown and in North America by Pantheon. *The No. 1 Ladies' Detective Agency* series is published in the UK by Abacus and Polygon and in North America by Pantheon and Anchor.

15 Writing for Children

Philip Pullman

Children's fiction often deals with the clash between good and evil. In the case of Philip Pullman, however, the crude dichotomy is more evident in the debate surrounding his work than in the stories themselves.

First, there is Pullman the saint. *His Dark Materials*, the dazzling trilogy set in parallel universes, has been hailed as the best work of children's fiction, if not any fiction, in decades. Whereas adults who read *Harry Potter* can feel justifiably embarrassed, those who devoured *Northern Lights* (*The Golden Compass* in America), *The Subtle Knife* and *The Amber Spyglass* need feel no shame. The books do more than just tell a cracking story, populated by a vivid cast of characters in a fantasy world of great imaginative richness. They are also steeped in ideas, exploring the difference between innocence and experience in an ethically complex universe.

Then there is Pullman the sinner. *His Dark Materials* is a deeply moral work, but it is also one which deals with ethical grey areas, criticizes the church, and has a child murderer, witches and a habitual liar among its cast of leading characters. The *Catholic Herald* has called his books the stuff of nightmares and worthy of the bonfire. Sarah Johnson, in *The Times*, claimed Pullman's heroes were 'Strong, clear-eyed children [that] have a natural purity that defeats all and clears a path before them rather like Hitler might have envisaged his Hitler *jugend* doing.' Peter Hitchens, writing in the *Mail on Sunday*, called Pullman the most dangerous author in Britain.

It is ironic that it is Pullman's refusal to simplify the difference between right and wrong that is probably the main reason why critics are queuing up to judge his fiction according to just these simplified criteria. He sees no reason to compromise on key aspects of his writing just because he is aware that much of his readership is young.

'I don't think it modifies the seriousness of the ideas, the intellectual reach,' he tells me down the telephone, from his Oxford home. 'The thing that I'm aware of when I think of the children's audience is that they don't know as much as adults. They're not less intelligent, they're not less willing to think about big things, they're not keener to take refuge in happy stories about fairyland. The only difference that affects the way I write is that I'm conscious that young readers don't know as much about the world as grown ups. For example, if you have a question that touches something like politics, the way politicians work, you just have to explain it a little more clearly so that younger readers won't be left behind.'

When it comes to the moral dimensions of his stories, this means a refusal to present the world in schematized black and white. Pullman has repeatedly said that he is a storyteller, not a preacher. But in his Carnegie Medal acceptance speech he also acknowledged that 'All stories teach, whether the storyteller intends them to or not. They teach the world we create. They teach the morality we live by.' Given this, does he not feel any kind of special responsibility, knowing that a lot of his readers are young?

'I do feel a responsibility,' he replies, 'but I think if I were writing a book whose expected audience were purely adult I would feel a similar responsibility. In a piece I wrote on responsibility I quoted Dr Johnson: "The only aim of writing is to enable the reader better to enjoy life or better to endure it." I think if you're going to write a book that is going to make the reader think "Well, life is shit and miserable and you're going to die in great pain and suffering," you're not doing much good. That is a sort of responsibility and I do feel it, but it isn't only because I write for children.'

Those who claim that Pullman has abdicated this responsibility point to incidents in the books which can easily be made to look morally dubious.

'What I'm chided with occasionally is showing that children do violent things and violent things happen. My response is always to say: look at the tendency of the book as a whole. Don't take this incident or this page or this chapter and say this is what it's all about. What is the story as a whole teaching?

'Stories always teach whether we intend them to or not. I think that is true. What they teach is the temperament of the writer. If that is a sanguine and hopeful one, that is what they'll teach. If it's a sour and melancholic one, full of hatred and pessimism, that is what they'll teach as well.'

His Dark Materials also deals with the subject of sex and sexuality in a subtle and interesting way. Throughout the book we're never told anything explicitly sexual about what goes on, even though to adult readers there are many obvious sexual undercurrents. Pullman gives as an example a passage at the end of *Northern Lights*.

'We have a scene where Lyra is watching her parents, Mrs Coulter and Lord Asriel, as they talk together, and their dæmons are playing with each other in a way which at once strikes adult readers in a sexual way. A child wouldn't see this and would only notice the strange, tender ferocity of the way they're playing together, and would sense the intensity of feeling but not all the implications of what that means. An adult reader, looking at that, would be able to interpret it differently. Generally, whilst children might be aware of deep undercurrents of feeling, they won't know what they are or where they're going to lead, or indeed whether they're good or bad, or whether they're going to have an effect. Children are just aware of the depths and currents of feelings, and the presence of more powerful things that they yet have the ability to grasp.'

The lack of knowledge children have about sexual relations is what makes Pullman avoid explicit sexual references in the trilogy.

'I think that's one of the advantages of having a young readership,' he explains. 'There are various ways of dealing with the issue of sexuality when you're writing a book that's going to be read by young people. You can be completely upfront and frank as, for example, Melvyn Burgess is in his new book *Doing It*, which is much more deliberately for older teenagers. You can be adult about it and simultaneously come over all sort of modernist and coy and avoid treating it directly, but with allusion, metaphor and all that sort of stuff. I've always thought that's rather a feeble way out. It's rather like saying if you're a very clever reader you can have some sex, but if you're rather dim then you're not entitled to any. It's like the old idea of the duchess who said sex was far too good for the working classes.

'I find it easier just not to deal with the physical descriptions of it. You can imply a feeling much more strongly if you don't describe it directly. Some of the Hollywood films made under the Hays code are much more sexy, actually. You can get to the point when the touch of a hand on another hand is the sexiest thing that you can possibly imagine because of the reticence that has to hang over the rest of it. I find that a positive artistic advantage.'

It is not just that Pullman doesn't describe the sex lives of his characters. He sometimes does not know himself what they get up to. For example, at a key moment when two characters fall in love, he says, 'I took my attention away. I thought they deserved some privacy.'

He is even less in the position of the omniscient narrator in the case of Balthamos and Baruch, two angels who to this reader and many others appear obviously to be a homosexual couple. Pullman, however, knows only as much as we do about their sexuality.

'Balthamos and Baruch appeared to me at the very end of *The Subtle Knife*,' he explains. 'I hadn't known they were going to turn up before they did. Suddenly, at the end of this book, Will is aware of these other presences, who say, "Come on, we must get to Lord Asriel," "Come on, we must do this." I sort of left it at that and was rather puzzled myself by the appearance of these two and I didn't know who they were or what they meant until I began to work out *The Amber Spyglass*.

'Then it became clear that they were angels, that they were both male and that they loved each other. But I didn't know any more than that. It certainly wasn't included to make a political point about the desirability or naturalness of homosexuality or anything of that sort.

'Of course, they have been interpreted by some people as being obviously gay. Some critics have said that this is disgraceful and that I am in effect besmirching the whole idea of angels and spirituality. One chap in particular I remember wrote rather sniffily that he didn't think my gay angels were any good at all. Other critics who happen to be gay have said that they are good. But I don't call them gay at all. I don't use the word homosexual or anything else. I just present them as two beings, who happen to be male, who love each other. That's all. I don't know any more than that. I don't know if they have any sort of physical relationship because that's one of the things I haven't explored. Another is how dæmons are born. Occasionally a child writes to me and asks how they are born. "I don't know," is the answer. I haven't looked into the gynaecology of dæmons any more than I have the physical sexuality of angels.'

It is perhaps not surprising that Pullman can't himself provide a clear interpretation of the meaning of everything in his books, for such a one-to-one relationship between stories and their message is the stuff of allegory, rather than the complex metaphors Pullman works with.

'Allegory is terribly dull,' he says, 'because *this* means *that*, only that, always that and nothing else; whereas metaphor is a much richer and more open thing. It depends on what I am coming to think of as a political truth about reading, which is that it differs from writing; or interpretation differs from creation in this way: creation, whether it's writing, painting or whatever, is essentially despotic and autocratic in nature, because it's the work of one mind and one mind alone which has absolute power of life or death over this sentence, or that phrase or whatever it is. It brooks no interference and can only work if it's the one mind doing it. Reading, on the other hand, interpretation, is inherently, intrinsically democratic, because it is fundamentally a process of negotiation between the mind and the text, between the expectations you bring to it and the satisfactions and disappointments you take away from it. Maybe metaphor in that sense is democratic and allegory is autocratic because allegory says this is what it means and nothing else. It's a great mistake to import the kind of political structure appropriate to one activity into the other. It's a very bad idea to impose one single reading on a text: this, and this only, is what it means. Similarly, it's a bad idea to get a bunch of people together to write a novel. It never works.'

Pullman's preference for metaphor over allegory is connected with his desire that children, as well as adults, should find their own meaning in his stories. And of course, children and adults will often not uncover the same things.

'Bruno Bettelheim, in his book *The Uses of Enchantment*, gave a very Freudian interpretation of famous fairy tales and said that children need to read these things, or need these stories read to them, because they help them to work through those family conflicts, Oedipal complexes and that sort of stuff. That may be the case, but what certainly isn't happening when a child experiences *Little Red Riding Hood* and undergoes a sort of cathartic exploration of the Oedipal complex is that the adult is guiding the child through, saying, "Now this you see is a phallic symbol, and this is a symbol of your childhood passion for your mother." Bettelheim very wisely said you don't ever explain this sort of thing to a child. Let them find their own meaning in the story. Let them interpret this in their own way.

'If you do look at these fairy tales again as an adult, it is striking that you see all sorts of things in them which you didn't see before because you're now grown up. A child hearing a story such as *Little Red Riding Hood* for the first time is probably thinking "Gosh there are wolves, isn't that exciting!" What the adult is thinking is "Oh my god, this is really a metaphor for child molestation. This wolf is a paedophile. I'd never noticed that before. How awful. I must never let my child go out again." And the child's thinks "Oh this is frightening, what's going to happen? Oh the wolf's eaten Granny!" And the adult thinks "I really mustn't tell her this story again." And the child thinks 'I hope she reads me that story again tomorrow because I like it!'

'All these different things are going on. It is probably true then that children have a different kind of relationship with metaphor, a different approach to it, a different way of internalizing it;

however, that's not something that I'm actually thinking of when I'm writing the story.'

Although Pullman believes that as readers children differ from adults only in what they know about the world, he is by no means sentimental in his view of them. Indeed, on his official website he says: 'I don't mean children are supernaturally wise little angels gifted with the power of seeing the truth that the dull eyes of adults miss. They're not. They're ignorant little savages, most of them.'

'This says something about the way I see children in contrast to the way in which they have often been portrayed in literature,' he explains. 'In particular, in the "golden age" of children's literature, roughly from *Alice* to E. Nesbit, including Barrie and *Peter Pan*, Kenneth Grahame, A.A. Milne and *Winnie the Pooh*, the state of childhood was viewed from the perspective of the rather jaded adult as being a beautiful, magical, wonderful time full of happiness and joy and there are toys, and the nursery fire and these lovely things which are lost and gone now. There was a sort of pathological nostalgia. This wasn't what it felt like to me to be a child. It's not the way my observations of children tell me they see themselves. It seemed to me even a partially sexualized view of childhood from an adult point of view; sexualized in that a great deal of it seemed to involve naked little children having a bath and being terribly sweet and making little comments to their nurses, diving into rivers and suddenly all their clothes fell off, that sort of thing. It was all rather grotesque and emotionally intense. I had a much more matter-of-fact feeling about childhood; and children are ignorant, they don't know very much, they can be grotesquely and horribly savage to one another and it seemed to me worth saying.'

Although Pullman is interested in dealing with serious ideas in his books, he seems to have an ambivalent relationship with philosophy. While he has endorsed Stephen Law's *The Philosophy Gym*, for example, he has also mocked a certain kind of academic philosophy in his hilarious *I Was a Rat*, and has approvingly cited Isaac Bashevis Singer's claim that there is more wisdom in a story than in volumes of philosophy.

'What he said was that events themselves are much wiser than any commentary on events,' he says by way of explanation. 'You just say what happened, who did what, who spoke, where they were and what happened next and leave it to the readers to interpret this and to find their own meanings and make their own connections. I think if we interpret it for them we are restricting it in ways which are profoundly unhelpful. They will find a better meaning than you will ever be able to tell them is there.'

Does he then think that philosophy has the demerit of giving you an account which strips away the interpretative part?

'Well, that would be a dangerous thing to say to a philosopher,' he replies. 'It would also be far too large a thing to say, because you then have to say which philosophy, what you mean by philosophy, which particular volumes of philosophy and so on. I think what I mean is wisdom here, which is to do with the experience of living and the experience of being grown up and having gone through various things such as marriage and parenthood and bereavement. It's not technical knowledge. It's the sort of thing you get in older people. The idea of a clever child is not a strange thing. The idea of a child with the wisdom of an old man is grotesque. The child would be a freak. It's impossible to conceive.'

Perhaps then his reservations are rooted in the fact that in philosophy one can be clever without being wise (just check out any recent issue of an academic journal for proof), whereas a work of fiction, if it's just clever, won't stand up.

'Yes, that is true,' says Pullman, more in reflection than as a definitive answer. 'Perhaps that was what I was getting at.'

What then of the idea that Pullman is a danger to our children? From certain ecclesiastical perspectives, the idea is not as ridiculous at it might seem, for Pullman's *His Dark Materials* trilogy is extremely subversive of established religion. Maybe it is a bit odd that at the time of our interview the churches were continuing to fret about gay bishops while children were devouring his books. A serious case could be made that his books could have more of a negative effect on established religion than any kind of inclusion of gay clergy.

Pullman laughs at the suggestion. 'Yes, quite. Well they've got their heads firmly in these little tiny parochial issues while this great wind of change is screaming past their bottoms.'

The big surprise is that Pullman hasn't created more of a storm in America, where religion is taken much more seriously than it is in Britain. Brits typically look at a church and see the potential for a nice residential or pub conversion. Americans generally still prefer to see them as houses of God.

'It's still a bit of a puzzle for me,' admits Pullman. 'The books have done very well in America. *The Amber Spyglass* was on the *New York Times* bestseller list for six months, so quite a lot of people must have bought it. But I haven't heard a peep out of them. I think they're so upset about *Harry Potter* that they haven't got on to mine yet.'

And there is no anti-clerical, anti-established religion agenda in *Harry Potter*.

'No, but it mentions witchcraft and witches and with the literal way that these people understand stories, that must be saying that they're true and they're dangerous and you watch out. Karen Armstrong has the best explanation for this. She points out that people have forgotten the more subtle ways of reading and understanding: they've blurred the difference between *mythos*, whose province is meaning and analogy and story, and *logos*, which deals with literal description. They read everything – in the Bible, and everywhere else – as if it were *logos*, and had to be understood literally. A great deal of anxiety could be harmlessly short-circuited if people learned to read more subtly; but then I suppose a lot of excitement would go out of their lives, poor things.'

Fortunately, many others can read properly and in Philip Pullman they have someone who really does know how to write to feed their imaginations and their intellects.

Suggested Reading

The *His Dark Materials* trilogy is published by Scholastic in the UK and Del Rey in North America.

16 Artificial Intelligence

Igor Aleksander

When it comes to philosophy, 'I quite like being naïve,' says Professor Igor Aleksander, with a smile. The admission of such naïveté from one of the world's leading authorities on Artificial Intelligence (AI) may seem surprising, but should not be taken at face value. For Aleksander's 'confession' is really a self-deprecating way of saying that, as far as he is concerned, much philosophy of AI is neither here nor there. If you want to get to the heart of the issues surrounding artificial intelligence, don't ask a philosopher: ask an engineer. Igor Aleksander, for example.

'Let's say we had a desperate need to put a robot on the market that was conscious, something that could go up on Mars and be sufficiently conscious to avoid disaster in a way that is akin to what an astronaut would do in the same kind of situation,' says Aleksander, explaining the practical basis of his methodology. 'The question is, what do I have to put into this robot in order for it to be accepted that it is conscious, both by philosophers and by British Aerospace or NASA or whoever?'

Philosophers, of course, ask such questions all the time. But for them, such thought experiments are purely hypothetical. They don't get down to working out the details of how you would actually go about building such a robot, which is precisely what Aleksander and his colleagues do.

'You see, the philosopher sits down and just thinks about it,' he says. 'But she or he doesn't have the tools to think about it properly. Being an engineer, I have tools that are more than merely linguistic, which allow me to think about how this thing would be made. So, for example, if I were to design one, it would have a brain-like architecture where there is a chaotic interaction between two parts of its brain – a depictive part and a memory part – because that's what I think gives me my sense of the interrelation between perception and memory, and so on. Without my engineering training I wouldn't have been able to do that. The tools that an engineer uses when conceiving of things like this are probably from a bigger bag than one a philosopher might have.'

When his approach is so practical, it is not surprising that many philosophical niceties leave him cold. For example, when I asked whether his approach was based on the idea that understanding the nature of consciousness is not just a conceptual matter, but an empirical one, he paused before replying: 'I'm not used to the distinction between the conceptual and the empirical. I think there are a lot of things that are empirical and also conceptual. In fact almost anything I do is conceptual rather than empirical.'

However, it would be a mistake to think that Aleksander simply has a cavalier disregard for philosophy. He peppers his comments with references to Searle, Chalmers, Dennett, Hume and Descartes which shows that he understands their arguments about mind and consciousness as well as anybody. And although he is keen to stress how engineering moulds his approach, in two very interesting respects his methodology is philosophical through and through. First, he proceeds, like a phenomenologist, by analysing what it is to be first-person conscious. Second, he structures his arguments like Kant's transcendental deductions, starting with what we know to be the case about consciousness and then working out what else must be true in order for it to be possible.

Both of these methodological principles are evident in his explanation of how he answers his own question about what would make his Mars-bound robot conscious.

The methodology I use starts with the first person. In the science of consciousness there is this problem that you actually start with physical systems and then wonder how you could have a first-person view of them. I'm very happy to admit that you can't have that. So I start with the first person and say, why do I think I am conscious? I end up giving five major reasons for that, which I call the five axioms. The first has to do with the feeling that I'm an entity, a self, in an out-there world. In other words, I'm separated from the world and other selves in it. That's the first strong sensation that I have. The second is that I can shut my eyes and that sort of feeling doesn't go away. That's imagination, memory, the whole internal lot. The third thing, which is very important and not obvious, is attention. The trajectory that I take through life is based on my attentional strategies, and I'm aware of those but not entirely conscious of all of them. The fourth thing is that I'm capable of deciding what I want to do next, and most of the time I'm sort of perceiving, imagining and thinking about what I might do or say next. And the fifth one is an emotional evaluation. I might stop myself from saying something if I think, "Oh God, that's bullshit."'

Once that phenomenological analysis is done, he moves on to the 'transcendental deduction' of what is actually needed for a system to have all five features demanded by the axioms.

'Having done that, I then use my knowledge of engineering to ask what mechanical systems, informational systems, computing systems you would have to have and how they would have to be structured in order to have those properties as a natural character of a circuit, not something that the programmer put in.

'You come up with interesting answers then. The system has to be cellular, for example; it has to have certain forms of depiction of its sensory surfaces, in other words it actually internalizes the world as it is, rather than the world as it is seen; it has to have a dynamic character without which it wouldn't have imagination, or recall, it wouldn't have planning ability; it must have certain evaluative systems, which both come from experience and are innate and deal with the emotions. So we end up with a kind of kernel architecture which I have suggested must exist in anything that we're ever likely to call conscious.

'Now we have a vague feeling that things a bit like ourselves are conscious, that animals are conscious, that sort of thing. I'm suggesting in order to call such things conscious they have to pass those mechanistic tests. I would be very happy for this to become an eventual definition of consciousness: if it passes those tests, if I know it has those mechanisms, then I'm prepared to call it conscious.'

Many philosophers who talk about consciousness are exercised by the notion of qualia, that 'what it is likeness' of conscious experience. Yet there seems to be no room for this in Aleksander's axioms.

'Well, how do you distinguish an argument about qualia from an argument about consciousness? People have argued that qualia is a feature of consciousness. But when you look at how people talk about qualia, you find that it tends to be about consciousness. So in order to have qualia, you need the five axioms at least. I would say that there are no qualia in a system that doesn't have a good dose of the mechanisms related to those five axioms. There is no mystery if you ask the question what does an organism need in order to know what it's like to be an organism.'

Although Aleksander's approach starts with the first person, it is crucial to understand that, in a sense, it ends by leaving it completely behind. Consider, for example, the sceptical doubt that if, by some miracle, I could somehow occupy your consciousness there would be differences in how we perceived the world. Maybe your shirt would have a more or less vivid colour, for example. For Aleksander, this isn't a shocking sceptical doubt but just what you would expect.

'It comes as a surprise to me that people still talk about the inverted spectrum argument: how do I know that what's red for me isn't blue for somebody else? If you look at it from the axioms, that just doesn't make any sense at all, because the axioms suggest that there is no fundamental representation. There is no code for red, there is no code for green and blue. In fact we know that, in neurology, you couldn't look into somebody's brain and say that he is now seeing a red object. It could quite easily be that the neural function of what some guy calls red is the same neural function of what some other guy calls green. All that means is that there are no describable representations for these elements in the world. They are rather to do with the way in which the organism attends to the world, develops its own representations, and the representation for red is only meaningful in the context of one brain. It has no meaning at all in any other context. I agree with Dennett that what it's like to see red, for example, has a lot to do with the pigment in our eyes, with how this has caused firing in particular areas of the brain, and so on.'

The upshot is that since we can never put ourselves in the position of any conscious entity, the things that are specific to an individual's consciousness are not the concern of a general account of consciousness.

'But isn't it interesting that we still attribute consciousness to other human beings and animals, even though we can't possibly put ourselves in their place?' says Aleksander, in response to this summary of his position. 'Take an animal that you believe is conscious. You couldn't possibly say that it is conscious of the world in the same way that you are. And yet it is conscious. So I think one has got to qualify consciousness in some way: it isn't just there or not. I'm not conscious in the same way as you are, and I'm not conscious in the morning in the same way as I am in the evening.'

The importance of this for machine intelligence is that we should not expect AI to produce entities that are conscious exactly like we are conscious. But this should not then be taken as grounds for saying that they are not conscious at all.

'If I have this robot standing next to this human being and people say to me, "Well obviously it's not conscious because it's not conscious like a human being, even though it has a brain that is modelled on a simulation of a human being's brain," I would say it is conscious, because it has been constructed to be conscious in the way that we think a human being is conscious. But its consciousness is completely different to that of a human being. How is it different? Because its physical makeup is different, and its concerns, what it is conscious of, are very different from that of a human being.

'Suppose I have a discussion with this robot, and I say, do you enjoy kippers? It has got to come back to me and say, "Hey, don't be stupid, humans enjoy kippers, but what I need is another 500K of memory or something. I'd really enjoy that!" So having a discussion with a robot might tell us something about what it is like to be a robot. I don't know what it's like to be a machine. I don't know what it's like to be a bat. But I know what mechanisms are needed for a bat to know about being a bat, and for a machine to know about being a machine.'

Critics of AI programmes offer a variety of reasons why the kind of thing Aleksander does can't result in genuine consciousness. John Searle, for example, is convinced that, since the one place we know we have consciousness is in biological brains, understanding the biology first is essential for understanding consciousness. Until we get a grip on how our brains actually produce consciousness, machine-based research will never get beyond simulation. Aleksander disagrees, believing that work in biology and with simulations goes together.

'You don't understand things in isolation,' he explains. 'For example, we've done a lot of work on Parkinson's disease and what happens to visual consciousness in Parkinson's, namely that some sufferers lose it. Why should that be? Neuroscientists have no idea, because they don't have these kinds of more sophisticated engineering models that we have. That's why we work very closely with them and we say, look, this is a complex system we've analysed in this way, and that predicts that in certain forms of Parkinsonism there's going to be a distortion of visual awareness.'

Indeed, the fact that by running simulations, Aleksander and his colleagues have had great successes in mapping their models back onto actual brains to explain how they work, or why they fail to work, is perhaps the best evidence that his project is on the right track.

'It just happens all the time,' says Aleksander of this flow of understanding. 'My colleagues in the neurosciences department quite freely talk about evolutionary algorithms, chaotic algorithms and so on, because it helps them in describing what goes on in the brain. They learned this by working with people who are used to working with complex systems, not necessarily in biology.'

Nor is Searle's famous Chinese Room argument at all decisive against Aleksander. 'I think Searle was right about the Chinese Room,' he explains. 'But it doesn't work against the kind of things I'm doing and Searle would agree with that.'

This may come as a surprise to those who interpret Searle's argument as working against anything that is run on a digital system. But as Aleksander explains, 'You can't have much against digital processors, because if you do you object to the way the brain works. Neurons, on the whole, the way the neurologists see them, either fire or don't. Everything else that happens is a massive interplay between things that fire and things that don't.'

The crucial difference between the kinds of systems Aleksander develops and 'Chinese Rooms' is that Aleksander works with neural networks.

'The kind of artificial intelligence that Searle was talking about is a computing machine that runs somebody's programme for understanding language,' Aleksander explains. 'In a Chinese Room there is a guy who has lots of rules, but doesn't understand Chinese, doesn't read Chinese characters. As these characters come through, he looks up the memory, he looks up the rules, fiddles about, gets new symbols, throws them out – so where's the understanding? The programme isn't doing any understanding. It's just processing data that comes in and goes out. However, when we talk about understanding in an intentional sort of way, in a Brentano kind of way, then we are talking about something else, and the something else is that we have an engaged experience of the world through systems that are capable of engaging in a certain way. Any system which is capable of passing the five axioms is capable of engaging in this way in order to build up an intentional representation of what the world's like. That's why it's outside the Chinese Room.'

A simple-minded response to this is to say that AI systems still run on digital computers, and Searle makes the point that any system which is basically ones and zeroes is going to fall victim to the Chinese Room problem.

'Well, Searle just doesn't understand about virtual machines,' Aleksander responds. 'He's right about the storm argument, that if you simulate a storm in a computer it's not a storm, though it tells you about storms. That's fine and there's no disagreement about that. But you can have this storm in a virtual environment that sits inside a computer where it has the same effect on that virtual environment as the storm has in a real environment, and you can learn something from that. When you use a conventional digital computer to run a system based on the five axioms, then it is true that the machine can only become aware of a virtual world. But the relationship between it and its virtual world is pretty much like the relationship between me and the real world. Then there is the third partner in this kind of argument, which is the robot, which is an embodiment of something that is in a virtual world, and you move what's happening in a virtual world into a real world. Then that robot can have the same consciousness of the real world as I have, but from a different point of view.'

The key point here is that the AI systems that Aleksander is talking about are not the kind of linear, rule-following systems that the Chinese Room models, but systems which themselves learn and don't just follow pre-programmed algorithms. In such neural circuits, patterns of long and short term memory have been seen to emerge spontaneously as part of their function.

'That happens under certain conditions,' says Aleksander, 'and you have to know what those conditions are. They have to do with the connectivity of the network. Let's say you have a neural network where every neuron is sensitive to what other neurons around it are doing, and sensitive to some sensory input from the outside world. So the sensory input from the outside world kind of forces these neurons to depict whatever is being seen, and neurons learn – in other words, if they see that again, they are going to fire in that shape. But being interconnected to one another they also learn what the other neurons are doing, and so they learn a stable internal state.

'Now let's say this sensory input doesn't come in, there's just noise. Since a neuron may kind of look for inputs from other neurons in more or possibly equal preference to looking for input from the sensory input, it can get into a state where that thing is represented even if it doesn't come in. That's called the stable state of the neural network. If you look at the mathematics of these stable states, that belongs to the field of complex systems and the emergent properties of complex systems, because under certain conditions – for example, if that network is over-connected, if the neurons are looking for too many signals from too many neurons – it will never fall into that state. Whereas if it has very few connections with other elements, then we know it's going to be very stable, and it's going to have order on the edge of chaos.'

Given that there are such things as emergent properties of systems, might things like the desire for self-preservation or will to power emerge from the complexities of systems?

'That's slightly confused,' Aleksander replies. 'What emerges is the ability to make sense of the world. To do this, you need an emergent property – an engine that's going to allow people to make sense of the world is an emergent type system with emergent properties. But the sense itself – that you need to survive in the world, that you have a certain kind of body, that you exist, and so on – isn't emergence. It's the properties of beings able to make sense that are emergent.

'In terms of its content, the way a robot will make sense of the world will be different from the way that I make sense of the world. I have a need to survive, and I know what I have to do to protect my family – my system has evolved with particular reactions. None of those things are necessarily givens in a machine. But nevertheless a machine may well develop. This robot that is going to Mars might have to develop instincts in the Californian desert to allow it to preserve its existence on Mars. Of course, you'll probably say, okay, but that robot isn't conscious – it just doesn't have the same preservational character as a biological system. However, the mechanisms that would make it preserve itself on Mars are pretty much the same as the mechanisms that I have as a result of knowing that I am a vulnerable biological machine. It is just that it knows it's made of steel and has got certain protections, and so on, which means that it's not going to worry about the same sort of things as I do. If I could have a discussion with it, then it would probably say, "I bet you wish you had a bit more of my consciousness, where I'm conscious of being immortal unless someone does something terrible to me – pulls my plug, for example. As long as there's electricity, I'm going to live the way that I do. But you're not going to. On the other hand, you want to take over the world because you enjoy the power. But I don't know what to do with that kind of power, or with money."'

Aleksander's view is that intelligent machines will come to have emotions, indeed, that they need emotions. It's not entirely clear, then, why a machine with emotions, capable of spontaneous development, might not develop emotions with unsavoury aspects. Why is he confident that this won't happen?

'I'm not all that confident,' he answers. 'But, to be really basic about things, a lot of the problems that arise with good and evil have to do with conflicts. In exercising one's free will or whatever, you come up against others who are trying to exercise their free will. Now it is true that you could get a machine that would be able to get into a conflict situation with human beings, but those sorts of conflicts would be much more controllable in a machine than they are in human beings.'

Of course, many people believe that Aleksander is far

too optimistic about the prospects for genuine machine consciousness. Some of these objections are tough-minded philosophical ones. But there is also a more general unease that many have when they consider AI. They see it as an attempt to demystify human nature and reduce us to 'mere machines'. The objection has rhetorical force, but lacks an argumentative edge. And, in any case, for Aleksander, his work does not hollow out humanity at all.

'I'm not trying to strip away any mystery or wonder. The more we find actual physical models of what might be needed for consciousness, the more awe and wonder we have about it. That becomes particularly pertinent, as in the case of Parkinson's disease, if you have a distortion of your consciousness, for which you have to understand the causes otherwise you just get stuck in a bin with no chance of a cure. By having mechanistic explanations of where consciousness comes from, why it's helpful to us to survive, and what the engineering basis of that is, I think we're actually creating a knowledgeable awe and wonder about the mind that might even help those suffering mental diseases, rather than leaving them to the fates.'

Suggested Reading

The World in My Mind, My Mind in the World (Imprint Academic)
How to Build a Mind (Weidenfeld & Nicolson)

Index